Edmund Maturin

Thoughts on the infallibility of the Church : with special reference to the Creed of pope Pius IV

Edmund Maturin

Thoughts on the infallibility of the Church : with special reference to the Creed of pope Pius IV

ISBN/EAN: 9783337103378

Printed in Europe, USA, Canada, Australia, Japan

Cover: Foto ©Lupo / pixelio.de

More available books at **www.hansebooks.com**

THOUGHTS

ON THE

INFALLIBILITY OF THE CHURCH:

WITH ESPECIAL REFERENCE

TO THE

CREED OF POPE PIUS IV.

BY THE

REV. EDMUND MATURIN, A. M.

AUTHOR OF "THE CLAIMS OF THE CATHOLIC CHURCH," &c.

"Beloved, believe not every spirit, but try the spirits whether they are of God; because many false prophets are gone out into the world."

St. John's 1st Epistle, IV. 1.

HALIFAX, N. S.

PRINTED BY J. B. STRONG, BOOKSELLER, ETC.

1861.

THOUGHTS, &c.

THERE are two great principles which it is the duty of every Christian to maintain, and to preserve, if possible, in perfect harmony with each other. One of these principles is the Unity of the Church, and the other is the Truth of the Gospel. The former relates to the external communion of the visible Church of Christ, and it is violated by the act of voluntary separation from the religious society of which we are members, which, when effected without a just cause, constitutes the sin of schism. The latter relates to the purity of the doctrines taught by our Lord Jesus Christ and His inspired Apostles, which form the foundation of true religion, any departure from which is therefore an error, or, when it is an obstinate denial of some fundamental truth, amounts to a heresy. Now the great practical difficulty is to reconcile a certain class of *principles* with a certain class of *doctrines*—that is, to reconcile the perfect Unity and divine Infallibility of the Universal Church with the preservation of Scriptural and primitive Christianity in all its Evangelical purity. Both ought certainly to be held together, if that be attainable; but if not, the one must give place to the other. We ask then, in that case, which of them is to yield to the claims of the other?

It is evident that if any visible church is guilty, in her official capacity, of teaching false doctrines, and requiring all her members to believe and profess them, then they are no longer bound to remain in her communion, because the

true doctrine of Christ is the unchangeable rule of Christianity, which can never be altered or superseded by any
human authority. But the question is, whether it is possible
for the visible Church ever to depart from teaching the true
faith of the Gospel to such an extent as to require a reformation of her doctrines, and consequently to justify the separation of her members who are convinced of the necessity
of such reformation, while others refuse to acknowledge the
errors of their church. The Church of Rome maintains that
the Universal Visible Church of Christ is preserved, by a
special privilege conferred upon her by Almighty God,
from the *possibility of error* in all matters of faith; and,
therefore, that it can never be lawful for her members to
leave her communion under any circumstances, or to attempt any alteration in her established system of doctrine.
This special privilege is known by the name of the "Infallibility of the Church," and it is believed to consist in the
perpetual guidance of the Holy Spirit, directing and con-
trolling her in all her decisions. The Church of Rome
further identifies *herself* with the Universal Church, and
claims the privilege of Infallibility as her own peculiar prerogative; for though it has never been formally asserted
or defined in any of her public decrees, yet it is virtually
implied in all her proceedings, and strenuously held by all
her Divines, as the very foundation of faith. It is attempted
to prove this fundamental principle by certain arguments
which appeal to the reason and judgment of mankind,
and having succeeded in establishing this position, it follows that all the *doctrines* which she teaches are divinely
true, as resting upon the same *principle* of infallible authority. She does not, indeed, encourage an examination of
each separate doctrine on independent grounds of inquiry,
as such a process might lead to their rejection on account
of their apparent opposition to Scripture or to primitive

antiquity : but she regards it as sufficient to demonstrate the general principle of her divine commission and authority, which virtually includes all further details of doctrine and practice. And thus her whole religious system is contained in a single comprehensive proposition, which asserts that our Blessed Lord has founded One, Visible, Infallible Church on earth, which He eventually committed to the spiritual government of St. Peter and his successors in the See of Rome, and which is now commonly known by the name of the Roman Catholic Church.

The writer of the following pages must confess, with deep contrition and humiliation, that he was once deceived by the seductive claims of this system ; and, being resolved to act in accordance with his conscientious convictions, he joined the communion of the Church of Rome, which he believed to be the "One, Holy, Catholic, and Apostolic Church" of Christ ; and in consequence of this act, he felt himself under the necessity of separating from the communion of the Church of England, to which he had been strongly attached by early education and religious association, and especially by the sacred office of the Ministry, in which he had been happily engaged for many years. Since that time, he has had ample opportunit' 's for further experience, study, reflection, and prayer ; and after a long and painful mental conflict, he is compelled to acknowledge that the whole theory of Church infallibility, as it is now held by the Church of Rome, is a mere delusion of human invention, and especially so, as it is made the foundation of the most dangerous corruptions of the Gospel of Christ, in doctrine and in practice. As it was this view of the subject which, almost exclusively, decided him in favor of Rome, he feels it to be his peculiar duty to reconsider the grounds of his own convictions, by examining the proofs alleged for the general principle of infallibility, and then reviewing the practical effects of this principle, as exhibited in the modern Creed of the Roman Church. And may God, for Jesus Christ's sake, give us His Holy Spirit, that we may have a right judgment in these and all other doctrines of His revealed Word!

Before I enter upon the consideration of this subject, it may be right to advert briefly to the circumstances which have led to the present publication. It was in the month of November, 1858, that I joined the Roman Catholic Church in London, though it was only a few weeks previously that I had seriously commenced to devote my earnest attention to this study, and only a few days before that I finally decided on this step. It is true that I had some doubts on this subject in early life, but the impression produced on my mind at this time was of so powerful a nature as to lead me to act at once upon the immediate impulse thus communicated, as though I had received a direct revelation superseding the necessity of any further inquiry or consultation. I had, indeed, drawn up a paper, for my own private satisfaction, under the title of the "Difficulties of Romanism" containing a statement of the principal objections which occurred to me, in opposition to the doctrines and practices of the Church of Rome. I was anxious to have a full explanation and discussion of these several points, in conference with an eminent Divine of that Church, but as I had not the opportunity of doing so, I thought it unnecessary to enter into any further details as to the proof of each particular doctrine, regarding them chiefly as speculative difficulties, while I was satisfied on the great principle of the Infallibility of the Church. I shall here insert a copy of this document, which relates to the following inquiries.

1. To prove the Infallibility of the Church of Rome.

2. To prove that the Church of Rome is the only true Church of Christ.

3. To prove that the doctrines of the Church of Rome, known by the name of Apostolical Traditions, were really taught by the Apostles, as articles of faith.

4. To account for the fact, that these doctrines are either apparently contrary to Scripture, or entirely omitted in Scripture.

5. To account for the omission, or imperfect notices, of these doctrines, in the Works of the Primitive Fathers.

6. To reconcile the doctrine of the Pope's Supremacy, as founded on Matt. xvi. 18, with the fact, that various interpretations, inconsistent with that doctrine, were held by several ancient Fathers.

7. To reconcile the doctrine of Transubstantiation with the particular explanations of the doctrine of the Eucharist, as given by some of the Fathers.

8. To distinguish between true and false Traditions, with especial reference to the Millennium and to Infant Communion.

9. To reconcile the Catholicity of the Church of Rome with the independent existence, and extensive propagation, of the Greek and Eastern Churches.

10. To explain why the Infallibility of the Church should not belong to the Greek Church as well as the Latin.

11. To reconcile the doctrine of exclusive salvation in the Church of Rome with the promises of the New Testament, that whosoever believeth in Jesus Christ hath everlasting life.

12. To reconcile the difference between particular and general Councils, and to explain the reason why the former are fallible, and the latter infallible.

13. To reconcile the doctrine of the Inspiration of the Apocryphal Books of the Old Testament with the fact of

their rejection by the Jewish Church, and by some of the Christian Fathers.

14. To reconcile the Tridentine doctrine of Justification with the statements of St. Paul.

15. To reconcile the doctrine of the Sacrifice of the Mass with the statements of Scripture as to the one Sacrifice of the death of Christ.

16. To prove that the doctrine of the Seven Sacraments was held in the Primitive Church.

17. To prove that the doctrine of Purgatory is consistent with Scripture.

18. To reconcile the practice of worship in the Latin Tongue with the statements of St. Paul.

19. To prove the necessity of the practice of Auricular Confession.

20. To reconcile the Celibacy of the Clergy with the rules of St. Paul.

21. To reconcile the worship of Images with the Second Commandment, and with the Fathers and Councils.

22. To reconcile the practice of Communion under one kind with the institution of Christ and the practice of the Primitive Church.

23. To reconcile the Pope's Supremacy with the statement of Gregory the Great, about an Universal Bishop.

24. To reconcile the temporal Sovereignty over the kingdoms of the world, claimed by several Popes by divine right, with the exclusively spiritual Supremacy, which is now generally admitted by Romanists.

25. To reconcile the doctrine of the Immaculate Conception with the unchangeable nature of the Christian faith.

26. To prove the invalidity of Orders conferred by Bishops in the Church of England.

These questions still appear to me to be entitled to the most serious consideration, as I have never heard or read any satisfactory answer to them, and therefore it may be, perhaps justly, regarded as an extraordinary act of enthusiasm or infatuation, that I allowed myself to be carried away by my convictions on one leading principle, without perceiving the force of these objections in counteracting the practical development of that principle. I had adopted a religious system founded upon my own study of the Bible, though modified by the decisions of the Council of Trent, according to my interpretation of its Decrees and Canons, and thus, without any further private instruction or examination, I was received into the communion of the Church of Rome. At the same time I wrote a Pamphlet, stating the reasons which induced me to take this step, in the form of a Letter to the Parishioners of St. Paul's, under the title of "The Claims of the Catholic Church." This was chiefly written in London, before I had actually joined the Church of Rome, and after having laid it aside for a time, I was persuaded to publish it shortly after my return to Halifax, under the impression that the reasons which had convinced my own mind would prove convincing to the minds of others. This Pamphlet produced several replies from the members of different Protestant denominations, in answer to which I published another and more extended work, in defence of the principles contained in the former essay.

As my views on this subject have since gradually undergone an entire change, I feel it my duty to God and to His Church, publicly to avow that change, while I proceed to make some observations on those principles, in connexion with the facts, reasonings, and conclusions mentioned in them; for, though I am not conscious of any wilful misrepresentation, yet I am well aware that there is occasionally much exaggeration on some important points, which requires to be materially corrected in order to form a proper estimate of their force and value.

My chief difficulty was the history of the Protestant Reformation of the 16th Century. It is obvious that the great objection was this, that the very idea of a *Reformation* of doctrine was founded upon the supposition of a general corruption of Christianity throughout the whole Church of Christ in every country in Europe, during a long succession of ages, while the Reformers themselves were only fallible men, acting in opposition to the highest ecclesiastical authorities, and unable to agree among themselves on many important points of doctrine. Now it is evident that this objection derives its whole weight from the belief that the Church of Rome, during the middle ages, and up to the period of the Reformation, was the only true Church of Christ on earth, and consequently that she had never fallen into any error in teaching the pure doctrines of Christianity. If she had really erred by adding certain human corruptions to the primitive Faith, and imposing these corruptions as essential terms of communion on the consciences of all her members, then assuredly it was the duty of all faithful Christians to reject these corruptions, and to adhere firmly to the faith of the Apostles, even though by so doing they should be regarded as guilty of heresy and schism, by the corrupt Church which had sanctioned them. Such persons do not *separate* from *the Church*, but from the *corruptions* of the Church, and therefore the guilt of schism must rest, not with those who reject these innovations, but with those who introduced and perpetuated them in the Church, whether the period of their continuance may have been of long or short duration. For it is certain that the whole system of Christianity was delivered by Christ and His Apostles, 1800 years ago, to the primitive Christians ; the original revelation, in all its parts, was then completed, and therefore, if it can be proved that any doctrine has since been taught which was unknown to the primitive Christians, or contrary to the primitive Faith, it cannot be received as an essential part of the Gospel of Christ, it must be rejected as a human invention, however ancient may be the date of its introduction, or however generally it may be adopted among professing Christians.

It is on this principle that we are exhorted by an inspired Apostle to " contend earnestly for the faith which was once delivered unto the Saints " (St. Jude 3), and another Apostle declares that " though we, or an angel from heaven, preach any other Gospel unto you than that which we have preached unto you, let him be accursed " (Gal. i. 8) It follows, therefore, that if any body of men should now teach any doctrines and practices which were not taught by the Apostles, and endeavor to enforce them as necessary to salvation, such a body of men would fall under the anathema of the inspired Apostle, whatever may be their claims to the Apostolical Succession of Bishops and to a divine commission founded upon such succession. The test of truth is not the Apostolical Succession of Bishops, which is possessed by some corrupt Churches, but the Apostolical succession of *doctrine* in all its original integrity. Such a body of men may boast of an unbroken line of Pastors, succeeding each other by regular ordination from the days of the Apostles, and of their uninterrupted unity at every period of their history, as having never separated from any other visible Church on earth. All this may be very true, but if it can be shown that they have departed from the doctrine of Christ and His Apostles, such external advantages can form no compensation for the corruption of divine truth, and we are bound to reject their testimony as contrary to the Word of God. We fully admit that the Church of Rome has never formally separated from any other Church, but this alone does not vindicate her from the charge of schism ; for if it can be proved that she has corrupted the Christian faith by introducing new doctrines and imposing them on her members as necessary terms of communion, then it is evident that she is guilty of virtually departing from her own former faith, and separating from her own former communion ; and therefore those who adhere to the old faith are not guilty of schism in rejecting these innovations, even though it should involve them in the necessity of excommunication or separation from the visible Church which has sanctioned these errors. Truth is truth, whatever may be the external channels through which it is transmitted to us—it is always essentially the same, while these channels are widely different from each other. Divine truth ought indeed always to be held and taught, if possible, in strict accordance with external unity ; but if that be not possible, then the latter must give place to the former, from the very nature of the case ; for the true faith of Christ must always be held by the true Church of Christ, and if any doctrine be taught by a modern Church different from that taught by the Apostles, it cannot be true ; while if any doctrine be taught by the Apostles, it must be true, whether taught by a modern Church or not. These principles are, of course, fully held, in theory, by Romanists as well as Protestants, and therefore the controversy chiefly depends on the proof of the fact alleged by Protestants, that the doctrines of Christianity have actually been corrupted by the Church of Rome. There is, however, one fundamental principle

held by the latter, which, if true, precludes the necessity
of any proofs on this head, and forms an insurmountable
objection to the validity of any evidence that can be
brought forward on the other side. That principle is the
Infallibility of the Roman Catholic Church, which forms
an invincible prejudice against all further reasoning on the
subject. This proposition consists of two parts—first, that
the true Church of Christ cannot err in matters of faith;
and second, that the Church of Rome is the only true
Church of Christ on earth. It is evident, then, that this
principle, if well established, completely covers the whole
ground of controversy between the Roman and the Reformed Churches. Roman Catholics profess to believe
every article of their Creed, not because they are satisfied
of the truth of each separate doctrine by personal examination, but because these doctrines are all received on the
authority of their Church, which they believe to be the
only infallible teacher of divine truth. But on what
grounds do they believe that their Church herself is infallible? This is the great subject of the present inquiry, to which I now invite the serious attention of my
readers, and I would remind them of the language of the
inspired Apostle—" I speak as unto wise men; judge ye
what I say. Prove all things; hold fast that which is good."

Now it is quite true that if the Church *cannot* err,
then of course it follows that she *has not* erred; but
if the Church *has* erred, then it is equally certain that she
can err, and consequently that she is not infallible. The
former is the line of argument adopted by the Romanist,
the latter by the Protestant—the one argues from a *principle* against the admission of *facts* in evidence, the other
argues from an induction of *facts* against the truth of the
principle itself. Romanists argue, and very justly, that

if their Church be divinely infallible, then it is impossible to suppose that she could have ever erred in teaching the true faith of Christ, because she is always guided by the Holy Spirit of God, and therefore that all the alleged proofs of her errors are merely founded upon the private opinions of fallible men, in opposition to the divine authority of the Church. Protestants, on the other hand, compare the doctrines of the Church of Rome with the doctrines of the Bible, which is admitted on both sides to be divinely inspired—and from an induction of particular instances they assert that *some* of these doctrines are *not contained* in the Bible at all, while *others* are evidently *contrary* to the teaching of the Bible. They thus arrive at a result which is founded on the comparison of two important facts, and from this they conclude that the Church of Rome has manifestly erred in matters of faith, and consequently that her claim to infallibility is an unwarrantable presumption and an unfounded tradition.

This is simply the state of the question on this momentous subject, and it may be reduced to this brief inquiry— Whether is there stronger evidence to prove that the Church of Rome *cannot err*, or to prove that she *has actually erred?* This alternative includes the whole controversy, when we take into consideration the solemn consequences involved in it, in the reception or rejection of all the doctrines and practices which are founded by the Church of Rome on the principle of divine Infallibility.

But what is meant by the Infallibility of the Church? It must be observed that "the Church" is here used by Roman Catholic Divines in a peculiar technical sense, not as including the whole body of the faithful, either visible or mystical, but only the *representative* Church, the "teaching and judging" Church, that is, the legitimate

Pastors of the Church, the Apostles and their successors, or the Catholic Bishops in communion with the Pope. It is obvious that objections may be made to this restriction of the meaning of "the Church," which has led to much confusion on the subject. It is evidently contrary to the proper definition of the term, as well as to its scriptural meaning, as it is certainly never employed in the New Testament in such a sense ; and therefore it is necessary that this peculiar sense should be distinctly understood, in order to guard against the substitution of one sense for another, which is frequently the occasion of the most serious errors on this point. Let it be remembered, then, that "the Church," in connexion with this argument, really means the Apostolical Ministry, that is, the Pope and his Bishops, or rather, indeed, the former alone, assisted by a congregation or committee of Cardinals at Rome, to whom the government of the universal Church is practically confided.

It is well known, indeed, that questions of great importance have frequently been raised, not only by Protestants, but by eminent Divines of the Roman Church, as to the precise seat of Infallibility, whether as vested in the Pope himself, or in a General Council, or in the collective body of Pastors, or in the combination of them all. These questions have never been formally decided, or rather, indeed, contrary decisions have been given by General Councils, as the Council of Basil, in 1438, decided that the Pope was *subject* to the Council, (though the Ultramontane party regard these proceedings as schismatical,) while the 5th Lateran Council, in 1512, *reversed* this decision. However, it is now practically held that a general Council is unnecessary for the determination of controversies, and though no immediate inspiration or personal infallibility is ascribed to the Pope or to any individual Bishops, yet it is believed that all their public decisions, on matters of faith, are guided by the direction of the Holy Spirit, and binding on the consciences of all the faithful members of the Roman Catholic Church. We shall briefly consider, then, the principal grounds of this opinion of the Infallibility of the Church, or rather, of the Pope in Council. The proofs on which it is supposed to rest are chiefly derived from three sources—Reason, Tradition, and Scripture.

On the ground of Reason, the one conclusive argument which is alleged is that of *necessity*. That necessity is supposed to be founded on the very nature of faith, as a firm assent to divine revelation, which must therefore be conveyed to us through the medium of an infallible teacher—on the difficulty of distinguishing between truth and error by any other means, as appears from the different interpretations of Scripture held by Protestants—and on the consequences of rejecting this principle, as opening a door for all the abuses of private judgment, and thus leading to infinite schisms and endless disputes among professing Christians. On such grounds it is argued that there *must* be some infallible Judge of controversy appointed by Christ in His Church, and that this Judge must be some living authority who is invested with absolute power to decide all disput s on matters of faith in every age. Now we fully admit the necessity of an infallible Rule of Faith, and we believe that God has given us such a rule in the Holy Scriptures. But though this argument for the necessity of an infallible Judge has been so plausibly urged by Roman Catholic Divines, we may surely ask, where is the conclusiveness of this reasoning? Are we the proper judges of that particular kind of

evidence which God is bound to give us for the guidance of
our faith? Are we sure that it is really necessary that
every controversy which arises in the Church should be
decided? May not some of them be left open questions,
without any prejudice to the unity of the faith? But
further, cannot these controversies be decided without an
infallible Judge? The Church of England, in her 20th
Article, declares that "the Church hath authority in
controversies of faith," yet she does not lay claim to any
absolute infallibility in her decisions. We admit that
there must be authority in every Church ; but cannot this
authority be final and decisive without being infallible?
And surely, if there be really an infallible living judge of
controversy, it is of the utmost importance for us to be
provided with an infallible proof that there is one, and
who he is ; otherwise all speculation on the subject is
practically useless. There is not a word in all the Scriptures about a living and speaking infallible judge of controversy, to whom all Christians are obliged to submit,
though this is the very foundation of religion, according to
the Church of Rome ; and therefore we may surely infer
with much more modest submission, that, since God Him
self has made no revelation on the subject, the belief in
the divine appointment of such a judge is purely gratuitous.
We would, indeed, gladly admit the principle, if it
could be proved ; but as the reasons alleged for infallibility
appear to us so inconclusive, we are certainly not at liberty
to adopt the conclusion without a full conviction of its
divine authority. Yet the supposed proof of the existence
of such a judge is founded upon a general presumption of
the usefulness and expediency of such a tribunal, from
which it is argued that there *ought* to be one, therefore
there *must* be, and therefore there *is*. But, after all, sup-

pose we are satisfied that there is one somewhere, the question arises, who is this Judge, and where is he to be found? For if we cannot find him, it is of no use to know that there is one in existence. We are told that this Judge is the Church, that this Church is the Church of Rome, and that the Church practically means the Pope. But on what authority is the decision of the Pope to be regarded as the voice of the Church? We are referred to the promise of our Lord to Peter—"Thou art Peter," &c. Still, however, we cannot discover, by the exercise of private judgment, any connexion between this promise and the Infallibility of the Pope. There is nothing here about the Bishop of Rome, or St. Peter's successors in that See. This interpretation is entirely founded upon the authority of the Roman Church, and therefore the attempt is merely an instance of the sophism of "arguing in a circle." The infallibility of the Pope, as the living judge of controversy, rests upon the interpretation of the promise to Peter, while that interpretation itself rests upon the infallibility of the Pope, or the authority of the Roman Church. But, further, are we sure that an infallible Judge would certainly decide all religious controversies in the Church? The Church of Rome, which professes to have such a Judge, has not exercised this power to the present day, as she has still left undecided some of the most important disputes relating to the peace of the Church and the interests of religion. Whatever, then, may be said, *a priori*, in favor of an infallible living Judge of religious doctrine on the ground of supposed necessity, we cannot admit the conclusiveness of such arguments, as they are chiefly founded on abstract reasonings, which cannot form the proper ground of faith; and the most difficult of all controversies is to decide who is the infallible Judge of controversy, as the decision of the question rests upon the exercise of private judgment, and is therefore liable to all the uncertainty of Protestantism, while the conviction of its reality depends only on moral certainty, or rather a strong presumption or high degree of probability, which may be easily counterbalanced by internal evidence arising from the practical consequences of the admission of this principle. We are told, indeed, that it is impossible to secure perfect unity of doctrine among Christians without submitting their opinions to an infallible Judge. –But if God has not appointed any such Judge, it must be highly dangerous to adopt his decisions as the rule of our faith; and further, as we are convinced that his decisions are, in many important points, contrary to the Word of God, we feel bound to reject his guidance, as being only calculated to lead us into error. We are told that if all men would submit to his decisions, there would be an end of all disputes. True, there might be an appearance of perfect unity, cold as death, silent as the grave; but it would be the unity of darkness, in which all colors agree, the unity of error and not of truth, and we think it infinitely better to differ on some minor points than to agree in the profession of dangerous errors. We are reminded, still, of the analogy of temporal Courts, and of the absurdity of private men interpreting the Law in opposition to the Judge. We admit that the parallel would be complete, if the Pope could prove his commission from Christ as clearly as every Judge can prove his commission from his Sovereign. In every case of appeal, the Judge's authority to hear and decide the cause must be perfectly clear; but we deny that the Pope has any divine authority given him for this purpose, as the proof of it rests upon a principle which is itself the very subject of dispute, and therefore we must decline to accept his decision as a judge of controversy, which he has only acquired by right of usurpation.

It cannot be denied that the appointment of such a tribunal by divine authority would be, apparently, the greatest of all blessings in the Christian Church; but we are certainly not warranted in assuming the existence of this tribunal without the express declaration of Almighty God, and we are certain that Almighty God has never made any revelation on this subject, directly or indirectly, in His Holy Word. We are fully persuaded that God has given us a sufficient rule of faith, which consists of His written Word, contained in the Holy Scriptures; and while we thankfully receive all proper helps for the right understanding of His Word, we are compelled to reject the claims of the Pope as the infallible Teacher of the Church, because we are convinced that it is only a human invention, having no foundation in reason or in Scripture. The Holy Scriptures are acknowledged by all Christians— Romanists as well as Protestants—to be divinely inspired, while the Pope's authority is rejected by all Christians except the members of the Church of Rome. Here, then, we stand upon the broad and comprehensive basis of divine revelation. And, further, we know that God has promised to give His Holy Spirit to them that ask Him; and though we do not expect the gift of personal infallibility, yet we are fully warranted in believing that God will not permit those who humbly and sincerely seek His promised guidance, to be led into any fatal errors. And, moreover, to guard against the abuses of private judgment, we have the interpretation of the Primitive Church laid down in the Creeds and Articles of the Church of England, which form the most effectual safeguard against the innovations of earlier and later times. We are thus led to rest our faith upon the Word of God, interpreted by the Holy Spirit, as understood by the primitive Christians, and therefore we cannot acknowledge the necessity of an infallible Judge, as we are satisfied that it is a mere expedient for the preservation of external unity at the expense of divine truth.

But there is another argument which has been put forward in proof of the Infallibility of the Church, and that is Tradition, or the historical testimony of the Fathers on this point. It is alleged that the Church herself has always claimed this privilege, that the most eminent writers of the Church in every age bear witness to the fact that such a principle was held in their times, and that this circumstance forms a strong evidence of the truth of the principle. Now we might reply that this is no proof of the divine origin of any doctrine, as our faith is founded on the Word of God, and not on the opinions of the Fathers. But after all that has been written on the subject, there is really little or no evidence to be found in the Works of the Fathers in favor of the Roman dogma of Infallibility. Not one of them expressly asserts such a doctrine, while there are numerous passages in their writings which are absolutely inconsistent with it. They do, indeed, strongly insist on the principle of Church authority, and on the duty of obedience to the Pastors of the Church, in opposition to the innovations of schismatical teachers; but it is a very remarkable circumstance, that, in all their controversies with the heretics of their times, the Fathers never appeal to the decision of any living infallible Judge, much less to the Bishop of Rome, as invested with divine authority to determine all controversies of faith, which is a plain proof that they were totally ignorant of

the existence of any sole authority in the Church, and
that they could not have acknowledged the fundamental
principle of the Roman Catholic Church at the present
day. They wrote, in earnest and eloquent language, on
the Indefectibility of the Universal Church, and the special
promises by which she is secured from the possibility of
utter extinction by any earthly power; but they never
assert her absolute infallibility in all matters of faith, and
still less do they ever connect that infallibility with the
See of Rome, by virtue of any divine promise given by
our Lord to St. Peter and his supposed successors in that
See. They appeal to the Scriptures, and not to the Pope,
nor to any living authority, for the final decision of all
controversies, and in confirmation of their argument they
also frequently refer to the tradition or doctrine held by
those Churches which were founded by the Apostles,
which was certainly a strong presumptive proof among
those who lived so near the times of the inspired teachers
of Christianity; but those venerable writers of antiquity
are entirely silent as to the modern doctrine of the Infallibility of the Church of Rome. It is true that if we des-
cend a few Centuries and consult the Fathers and Schoolmen
of later times, we shall find a very general consent in favor
of the principles of Romanism; but this testimony comes
too late to be of any real service, as it is contrary to the
testimony of the Fathers in the early ages, which alone
can throw any satisfactory light on the doctrines held by
the Primitive Churches, which were founded and governed
by the Apostles and their immediate successors.

The Church of Rome, indeed, does not admit of any appeal
from her own decisions, except so far as they may seem
to favor her claims, either to the Scriptures, or to the
Primitive, or Catholic Church of former times, all of which

she regards as a dead letter without the living voice of an infallible interpreter. The only authority which she admits is that of the *present* Church, and it becomes, therefore, the more necessary to examine carefully the foundation of a claim which thus practically supersedes both the only record of the original revelation and the earliest historical interpretation of it. Accordingly, we find that some writers appeal to certain "motives of credibility," which they think sufficient to establish the divine authority of the present Church of Rome, without referring to any Scriptural evidence. These motives of credibility are explained to be substantially the same with those which were employed to prove the divine authority of the Jewish and Christian Dispensations, and thus the claims of the Church of Rome are said to rest upon the same foundation with those of Christianity itself. We are referred to the miracles, prophecies, and other evidences of the divine presence, which have been exhibited at various periods in the history of the Church, and especially in the time of our Lord and His Apostles. But how do these evidences prove the peculiar claims of the Church of Rome? It is well known that Protestants generally deny the reality of such miracles during the later ages of the Church; and even if this point could be unquestionably demonstrated, it cannot be shown that any miracles were performed to prove the Infallibility of the Church of Rome, even though individual members of that communion might be supposed to have been gifted with such a power for proving the truth of Christianity. But it is in vain to appeal to the miracles of Christ and His Apostles in proof of this point, as such an appeal evidently *assumes* the whole question, as it takes for granted two things which can never be conceded by Protestants—the one, that the Church of Rome is the Catholic

Church of Christ ; and the other, .hat she is the same, in doctrine, now as she was in the beginning of Christianity. According to this method, then, the only reason for believing the Roman doctrine of infallibility is her own assertion of the doctrine—that is, we must believe her to be infallible because she says so herself, and we must admit her veracity because it rests, upon motives of credibility which depend entirely on her own authority.

In close connexion with this method, we are frequently directed to certain external marks, or "Notes of the Church," by which she is supposed to be distinguished from all other bodies of professing Christians, independently of all scriptural evidence on the subject. It is evident that this inquiry assumes that there is One True Visible Church on earth, to the exclusion of all others, and that this Church is perpetually infallible—both of which positions require to be proved on independent grounds. Further, we are required to find out the *Universal* Church, before we know what is necessary to constitute a *particular* Church ; we are required to determine which is *the* true Church, before we know what is *a* true Church—though it is certain that *a true Church* is one which professes and teaches the *true faith* of Christ ; and yet this point is studiously kept out of view, because it involves the consideration of doctrine, which can only be ascertained from the Scriptures, and thus leads to the Protestant principle of Scriptural examination, in order to test the claims of a professing Church. For the true Universal Church includes all true particular Churches, and a true Church is one which holds the true faith, and the true faith can only be found by searching the Scriptures, as the original records of the divine revelation. This, however, will not suit the views of the Romanists :

they tell us that the true faith can only be found in the true Church, and consequently that the true Church must be found before we can find the true faith; and therefore they refer us to various outward signs or tokens, by which we are to find the true Church. In addition to those mentioned in the Nicene Creed, the most celebrated is Cardinal Bellarmine's enumeration, in which he reckons up Fifteen Notes of the true Church, by which he endeavors to prove that the application of these marks is conclusive in favor of the claims of the Church of Rome. These "Notes of the Church" are as follows:—1. The very name of Catholic and Christian. 2. Antiquity. 3. Duration long and uninterrupted. 4. Amplitude, or number and variety of believers. 5. Succession of Bishops in the Roman Church. 6. Agreement in doctrine with the ancient Church. 7. Union of the members with their head and among themselves. 8. Sanctity of doctrine. 9. Efficacy of doctrine. 10. Holiness of life. 11. Glory of miracles. 12. Light of prophecy. 13. Confession of adversaries. 14. Unhappy end of the Church's enemies. 15. Temporal felicity of the Church's defenders. But there are evidently two strong objections to this method: one is, whether these are really the *distinctive* marks of the true Church of Christ, as some of them rest only on the arbitrary selection of an individual writer, while others of them can only be admitted as probable signs of truth; and the other is, whether, in fact, these notes really belong exclusively to the *Church of Rome*, and how many of them are necessary to prove her claim, as several of them are certainly claimed and possessed by *other* Churches; and therefore the application of these notes can never lead to any satisfactory conclusion on the subject, as they can never prove that a *part* is equal to the *whole*, or that the *particular*

Church of Rome is the *Universal* Church of Christ.

We now proceed to the third method of proving the Infallibility of the Church, which is derived from certain passages of Scripture, and especially from the promises of our Blessed Saviour, recorded in the New Testament. Some controversial writers dwell almost exclusively on this method, as being best adapted for the conviction of serious Protestants, who admit the divine inspiration of the Scriptures; while others confine themselves entirely to the general considerations already stated, and thus avoid the appearance of arguing in a circle by attempting to prove the authority of the Church from the Scriptures, and then the Scriptures from the authority of the Church. And, indeed, it seems in vain to attempt the proof of the Church's infallibility in any other way than by an appeal to the written Word of God, which is acknowledged on both sides to be of divine authority. For in what other way can it be proved? Not on the ground of necessity, for Protestants do not see any such necessity, as they believe the Scriptures to be a sufficient rule of faith, without any living Infallible Judge. Not on the ground of tradition, for Protestants do not acknowledge its authority; and besides, they are convinced that, in point of fact, the claim is refuted by a genuine appeal to tradition itself. It remains, therefore, to examine the Scriptural evidence on this point. I feel this to be the more necessary in my own case, because it was this view of the question which chiefly produced such a strong conviction on my own mind. My submission to the Church of Rome was an act of private judgment, founded upon a particular interpretation of the promises of Christ, in connexion with some important facts in the history of the Church. I was led to believe, on probable evidence amounting to a full persuasion, that our blessed Lord had promised the gift of Divine Infallibility to His Church, and that the Church of Rome is the historical representative of that Church on earth at the present day. In the words of Chillingworth—"I reconciled myself to the Church of Rome, because I thought myself to have sufficient reason to believe that there was, and must be always in the world, some Church that could not err; and consequently, seeing all other Churches disclaimed the privilege of not being subject to error, the Church of Rome must be that Church which cannot err." But the question is, was I right in this conclusion? I certainly lay no claim to infallibility for myself, and if convinced of any error, I am quite ready to acknowledge and renounce it. Does, then, the Bible teach the doctrine of the Infallibility of the Church of Rome? It must be observed that no argument can be founded on any promises relating to "the Church," as employed in Scripture, because this word is evidently used in a totally different sense by the Roman Divines, as referring to the Apostolic Ministry instituted by our Blessed Lord. It is perfectly clear that this word is never used in this sense in the New Testament, as may be seen from a particular examination of all the passages in which it occurs. It will thus appear that, wherever the word is found in the *singular* number, and without restriction to a *particular* place, "the Church" means the whole body of God's faithful and elect children, who are washed from their sins in the precious blood of Christ, sanctified by the Holy Ghost dwelling in them, and who will be finally glorified with Christ in His heavenly kingdom. This is the only true "Church of God in Christ," consisting of "the election of grace," including all those who are in this life united to Christ by His Holy Spirit, and who will be hereafter saved in the Lord with an everlasting salvation. It seems evident, however, that when the word is used in the *plural* number, or in the *singular* with reference to any *particular* locality, " the Churches" mean the various visible societies of professing Christians in those places. Thus we read of the Church in Jerusalem, the Church in Antioch, the Church in Corinth, the Church of the Thessalonians, the Churches of Macedonia, the Churches of Galatia, the Churches of Judea, the Seven Churches in Asia, and afterwards of each one of them in particular. The aggregate of all the various local Christian Societies in the world is described under the name of " all the Churches," but it does not appear to be ever included in the general name of " the Church," in its scriptural sense, though it evidently was at an early period in ecclesiastical history. There is certainly no intimation in the New Testament, from which it could be inferred that our blessed Lord ever intended to found One Visible Universal Church on earth, although all the Churches were virtually united in one communion by the same common bonds of faith in the Lord Jesus Christ, and love to all the Saints. Still less can we find any description of the Church under the idea of a Universal Spiritual Monarchy, governed by one visible Head, as the Vicar of Christ on earth. It is true that, as a member of the Church of Rome, I formerly held this to be the true interpretation of Matthew xvi. 18, 19. This interpretation, however, was not founded upon the evidence of the passage itself, which appeared to me capable of a more easy explanation from the New Testament history, but upon the supposed infallibility of the Church of Rome, which has affixed this sense to the words, in accordance with her own doctrine of the Supremacy of the Pope. The promise is, that " the gates of hell shall not prevail against the

Church of Christ." Now " the gates of death," or *hades*,
(according to the Greek expression), simply means the
dominion of death or the unseen state of separate souls,
and consequently the idea referred to is the promise of
immortality or eternal life. " The Church of Christ "
may be understood either as the *visible* body of professing
Christians, or as the ... cal body of Christ's chosen
people. In the former sense, it is a promise of the per-
petuity or indefectibility of the Church, and thus conveys
the assurance that the profession of Christianity should
always continue to exist on earth ; while in the latter sense
it contains a promise of the perpetual preservation of His
faithful people, and their final deliverance from the power
of death by a glorious resurrection to eternal life, according
to the promise of Christ (John x. 28). Besides, the promise is made to *the Church* of Christ—that is, to the *whole
body* of true Christians, and not merely to the Apostolic
Ministry, as applied to the Bishops in communion with the
Pope ; and therefore this passage proves nothing on the
subject of the Infallibility of the Church of Rome.

There are two other passages of a similar nature, which
are frequently quoted in proof of the same point, and
they afford a remarkable example of the same kind of
sophistical reasoning, founded on the ambiguous meaning
of the word " Church," which occurs in them both. Indeed, these passages are regarded as so conclusive in favor
of the doctrine of the Church of Rome, that they are inserted as proof texts in the very " Act of Faith," in which,
after reciting certain dogmas, it is added—" I believe these
and all other articles which the Holy Roman Catholic
Church proposes to our belief, because Thou, my God, the
Infallible Truth, hast revealed them, and *Thou hast commanded us to hear the Church, which is the pillar and*

ground of the Truth." The first of these is Matthew
xviii. 17—" Hear the Church." Now it is evident from
the preceding context, that this passage has no reference
whatever to the authority of the Church in determining
controversies of faith, as it relates not to any question of
doctrine, but of discipline, or to some occasion of dispute,
founded on personal injury, between two private Christians.
" If thy brother shall trespass against thee, go and tell
him his fault between thee and him alone : if he shall
hear thee, thou hast gained thy brother " (v. 15). Should
this course not prove satisfactory, the next step is this—
" If he will not hear thee, then take with thee one or two
more, that in the mouth of two or three witnesses every
word may be established" (v. 16.) Should this arbitra-
tion fail, the final appeal is directed to be made to " the
Church." " If he shall neglect to hear them, tell it unto
the Church ; but if he neglect to hear the Church, let him
be unto thee as an heathen man and a publican."
Now what is " the Church " here mentioned ? Every one
knows that the word properly means an assembly or congregation, and in this sense only it can be understood in
this place. It cannot surely mean the Universal Church,
whether visible or mystical, as it is absurd to suppose that
our Saviour could have intended to refer every private
difference to the decision of a general Council of the
Church in any sense, and therefore, according to the natural
meaning of the climax, ascending from one, two, and
three to a greater number, it must relate simply to
the local society or congregation, whether collectively or
representatively, of which those two individuals were
members ; and thus we find the same rule particularly laid
down by St. Paul with reference to the congregation of the
Corinthian Church (1 Cor. vi. 1—6.) This text, then,

relates, not to matters of *doctrine*, but of *discipline*—not to the *Universal* Church, but to a *particular* congregation—not to the *Bishops*, but to the *people*; and therefore, if it proves the Infallibility of the Church, it must prove the Infallibility of every Christian congregation in the world, and consequently, as this proves too much, it proves nothing at all on the subject of Infallibility.

The other passage, so often triumphantly quoted, is 1 Timothy iii. 15, in which it is understood that "the Church of the living God" is described as "the pillar and ground of the truth," and consequently infallible in all her determinations of doctrine. But, in the first place, it is by no means certain that this expression relates to "the Church" at all, as it may be equally applied, in its grammatical construction, either to Timothy himself, in the former part of the passage, or, without any violence to the original, to the "mystery of godliness," in the following verse. According to the former interpretation, the Apostle was giving directions to Timothy "how he ought to behave himself in the house of God," which he explains, parenthetically, to be "the Church of the living God," and then continues his exhortation to him to act in his high position as "a pillar and ground of the truth." Indeed, there are two important objections to the common view, which refers these words to the Church—one is the *confusion of metaphor* which it involves in describing the Church both as a "house" and as a "pillar" in the same sentence; and the other is the *omission of the Greek articles* before the latter terms in the sentence. We find that the name of "pillars" is applied in Gal. ii. 9, to leading *individuals* in the Church, James, Cephas, and John; and again, in Rev. iii. 12, to the individual victor in the Christian conflict, but it is never applied to any collective

bodies of men. But, even supposing that the Church is called
"the pillar and ground of the truth," the allusion is probably made to the pedestals, on which statues were raised,
to be exposed to public view, and this is indeed the proper
office of the Church, as a "candlestick" for the diffusion of
divine light and truth, "holding forth the Word of life"
as "a witness and a keeper of holy Writ." But further,
the Church here mentioned is not the *universal* Church,
but the *particular* Church of Ephesus, of which Timothy
was Bishop, and therefore the expressions apply to every
particular Church in the world, and prove nothing on
the subject of Infallibility. Now it is certain that this
very Church of Ephesus, which the Apostle calls "the
pillar and ground of the truth," did afterwards fell into
corruption and apostacy, and is now utterly extinct.
But a few years afterwards, she was solemnly warned as a
fallen Church by our blessed Lord, who threatened to
"remove her candlestick out of its place." (Rev. ii. 4, 5.)
Besides, these terms are applied to *the Church*, or the *whole
company* of Christians in any place, and not to the Bishops,
or Pastors of the Universal Church. Is it not evident,
then, that there is a gross imposition in the application of
these two texts from their obvious meaning, to prove the
doctrine of Roman Infallibility? It is surely a manifest
attempt to deceive the people by the mere sound of
words, employed in different senses in the premises and in
the conclusion, while it is plain that "the Church" in
these passages of Scripture means "the Laity" as distinguished from "the Clergy," and in the Roman argument
it means "the Clergy" as distinguished from "the Laity."

But though these texts are thus entirely perverted from
their true sense, there are some others which have a more
direct bearing on this subject. We need not refer to the

Prophecies of the Old Testament, which are frequently quoted on this point, because it is evident from an attentive examination of the contexts of those passages, that they do not relate to the Christian Church at all, but chiefly to the Jewish nation after their future conversion and restoration. Such are Isaiah ii. 2—4, lix. 21, Jer. xxxi. 31, and Hosea ii 19, 20. One of the principal texts in the New Testament is the promise of our Lord to His Apostles, "Lo, I am with you alway, even unto the end of the world"—(Matt. xxviii. 20.) Granting that this promise extends to the *successors* of the Apostles in all future ages, still there is nothing here about the Infallibility of the *Roman* Church. For who are the successors of the Apostles? Even supposing that none but the Bishops are included in this description, still there is no limitation to the Church of Rome, and therefore it must include the Church of England as well as every other branch of the Universal Church. Nor is there any Infallibility implied in the promise of Christ's perpetual presence. The same promise was frequently given to individual faithful servants of God, as well as to collective bodies, and yet surely it cannot be alleged that, on other occasions, there is any Infallibility conferred by the promise, "I am with you," &c. Our blessed Saviour promised, "where two or three are gathered together in My name, *there am I* in the midst of them," (Matt. xviii. 20,) and surely it cannot be inferred that every little company of praying Christians is rendered infallible by virtue of this promise. If this were the meaning of the promise before us, then each *individual* successor of the Apostles would be personally infallible to the end of the world. And besides, it cannot be denied that there is a *condition* annexed to the promise—"teaching them to

observe all things whatsoever I have commanded you."
When this condition is neglected, the promise fails
—it is not connected merely with Apostolical succession, but with Evangelical doctrine, and therefore it is
not a promise of absolute Infallibility exclusively belong-
ing to an uninterrupted succession of individuals in the
Episcopal office, but it is a promise of gracious assistance and divine protection, arising from the presence of
Christ with all the faithful ministers of His Gospel in every
age of the Church.

Another Scriptural proof of the doctrine of Infallibility is founded on our Saviour's last Discourse with
his Disciples, which contains the promise of the Holy
Ghost as the divine and infallible Teacher of the Church,
instead of Jesus Christ Himself, John xiv. 16, 17, 26
xvi. 6, 13. Here again, we observe that these promises
are conditional, as depending on the love and obedience of Christ's professing disciples—"If ye love Me,
keep My commandments." But it is evident also, that
some of these promises are *personal* and cannot be
applied to any others but the Apostles themselves, for it is
said that "He shall teach you all things, and bring all
things to your remembrance, whatsoever I have said unto
you." "He will show you things to come," enduing
them with the gift of prophecy, in predicting future events,
which can only apply to immediate *inspiration*. It is said,
indeed, that "He shall abide with you for ever," and
thence it is argued that the promise must extend to their
successors in the government of the Church for all time to
come. It is by no means clear, however, that this conclusion is just, as some commentators are of opinion that the
words " for ever " may refer only to the natural lives of the
Apostles, or to the perpetual authority of their inspired

writings. But even if it be true that it includes their successors, there is not the slightest proof that it applies to the Church of Rome more than to any other part of the Universal Church, nor does the gift of the Holy Ghost confer Infallibility without some special promise to that effect, which is certainly not expressed in this passage. The Holy Ghost is given to all true believers, who are thus made " the children of God by faith in Christ Jesus " —they are " sealed with the Holy Spirit of promise," and their " bodies are the temples of the Holy Ghost." Without this no one can be a real Christian, for " if any man have not the Spirit of Christ, he is none of His." Yet this precious gift certainly does not make individual Christians infallible, or exempt them from all possibility of error— there is no proof that our Lord is here addressing his faithful disciples, in their official capacity, as inspired Apostles or representatives of the Apostolic Ministry to all future ages, and certainly the same language may be applied to them in a general sense, as representing all the members of Christ's mystical body till the end of the world.

Another passage, frequently quoted, is Eph. iv. 11—14, which has been supposed to prove that there is an infallible succession of Apostles, Prophets, &c. till the end of the world. But there is nothing said about the *infallibility* of these guides, as they include ordinary " pastors and teachers," and there are certainly no inspired Apostles or Prophets now in the world; besides, this event is described as *past*, when he says "He gave some," &c. Yet it is not certain that St. Paul speaks here of any *succession* at all, as the words "till we all come," &c. seems rather to refer to the time during which the Church is to be edified by the instructions of the Apostles, &c. which are now to be found only in the same writings. It is almost unnecessary to refer to such passages as Luke x. 16, and Heb. xiii. 17, which are often quoted to prove the Infallibility of the present Church of Rome; but the former text relates to the seventy disciples, who had certainly no connexion whatever with the Church of Rome; and the latter relates to the ordinary Pastors of the Church, who are fallible men, to whom our obedience is limited by the Word of God, but neither of them has any exclusive reference to the Church of Rome or the claims of her Clergy.

We have thus taken a general view of the principal arguments which have been advanced in proof of the Infallibility of the Church, or rather of the collective body of Bishops in communion with the See of Rome, and I think it must be admitted that they are utterly inconclusive. It is evident, however, that, whatever degree of force there may be in these arguments, they prove nothing in favor of the Church of Rome in preference to any other Church; the very same arguments, being founded on general principles and promises, would equally prove that Infallibility belongs to the Greek Church, which is said to claim this privilege as well as the Latin. It is manifestly absurd, however, to maintain the principle of two infallible Churches, at variance with each other; the Infallibility, as well as Supremacy, must be vested in one Church only; and therefore the Latin Church, with the view of monopolizing this privilege, has consistently cut off all others from the unity of the Catholic Church, and pronounces them to be involved in the guilt of schism, because they refuse to recognise her claims to Universal Supremacy. But, after all, how infinitely precarious is the attempted proof of the Infallibility of *any* visible Church on earth? how very uncertain is the conclusion derived from it in favor of the Church of Rome! Let us look at the analogy of the

Jewish Church. It was the only true Church of God on
earth, founded by the Almighty Himself, and established
with miracles and prophecies, accompanied with the promise of the abiding presence of God's Spirit among the
children of Israel—" And I will sanctify the tabernacle
of the congregation, and the altar : I will sanctify also both
Aaron and his sons, to minister to me in the priest's office.
And I will dwell among the children of Israel, and will be
their God. And they shall know that I am the Lord
their God, that brought them forth out of the land of
Egypt, that I may dwell among them : I am the Lord
their God." (Exod. xxix. 44—46.) " For now have I
chosen and sanctified this house, that my name may be
there for ever ; and mine eyes and mine heart shall be
there perpetually." (2 Chron. vii. 16.) "According to
the word that I covenanted with you when ye came out of
Egypt, so my Spirit remaineth among you ; fear ye not."
(Haggai ii. 5.) It had a perpetual succession " a
divinely instituted Priesthood of the order of Aaron, and
the sentence of the High Priest was to be final in all
matters of controversy relating to civil causes—" And the
man that will do presumptuously, and will not hearken
unto the priest that standeth to minister there before
the Lord thy God, or unto the judge, even that man
shall die : and thou shalt put away the evil from Israel."
(Deut. xvii. 12.) Yet it is evident that there was no
Infallibility conferred upon the Jewish Church, except so
far as it adhered to the written Law of God. The great
body of the nation fell into idolatry at various periods.
They were divided into different and opposite sects in the
time of our Saviour. And finally, it is a solemn and
startling fact, that our Lord Jesus Christ was condemned
and crucified by sentence of the only visible Church of God

on earth, as represented by the High Priest and great Council of the Jews. What confidence, then, can we have in the decisions of the Pope and his Council at Rome? And if there is so much uncertainty in the *foundation*, how much more uncertainty must there be in the doctrines established on this supposed Infallibility, besides the particular evidence against each separate doctrine! We are told, indeed, of the great advantage, in point of certainty, which is possessed by the members of an Infallible Church. But it must not be forgotten that the mere assertion of Infallibility, however confidently claimed, does not make any Church infallible. All depends on the conclusiveness of the reasons advanced to prove her Infallibility. These reasons cannot produce an infallible assurance of the Church's Infallibility in the mind of any one; they cannot remove all doubts on the subject, and therefore the Romanist can have no advantage over the Protestant as to the grounds of conviction of the truth of his religion, as it is impossible to arrive at a *certain conclusion* from *uncertain premises*. How am I more certain of my faith in the Church of Rome than in the Church of England? Because, it is said, I belong to an Infallible Church. But, supposing this to be true, still it does not make me infallibly certain of the truth of her doctrines, unless I have an *infallible certainty* of the Infallibility of the Church herself, which, I confess I have not. I have nothing but a *moral* certainty of it, founded upon probable evidence, and I can have the same kind of certainty in the Church of England. I must confess, indeed, in my own case, that it was this desire to obtain a more absolute certainty of faith which formed one of the predisposing causes which operated strongly in my own mind in favor of the system of Romanism, and I believe it is this which constitutes the peculiar attractions of the system to many minds conscious of their own weakness, and longing for an infallible authority in the interpretation of divine truth. This is well expressed in the following eloquent passage from a sermon by a living clergyman :—" What is that strange charm and witchery of this system, by which it has held in subjection in times past, by which it bows to subjection in our own day, so many a noble intellect, in spite of all the grossness of its errors and the monstrous and incredible character of its superstitions? Is it not this—that, claiming the revelation of the *sign*, it professes to give that *certainty*, that absolute freedom from all doubt in matters of faith, which men so earnestly desire? Is it not that, to minds worn out with the strife of controversy and the agony of doubt, it offers repose, relief from all the painful effort at deciding for themselves questions for which the human intellect can never find a satisfactory solution? To souls exhausted with the feverish anxieties of freedom, it offers the rest of despotism. To the weary and heavy laden, borne down with the burden of their own doubts and difficulties, Rome speaks ever, in cruel and deceitful parody, those comfortable words of Christ, " Come unto me, and find rest for your souls." Still does she stand, the false representative of Christ by the well-side, where come those who thirst for *truth*, and telling them ever that they " have nothing to draw with, and the well is deep," bids them ask of her, and she will give them water, which if they drink of, they shall never thirst again." This witness is true ; it describes the secret of that mysterious fascination thrown over the minds of men by the extravagant claims of the Church of Rome ; and therefore, instead of indulging a romantic sentiment, it becomes our duty calmly and soberly to examine attentively the

foundations of this claim to infallibility. It is evidently
incorrect, then, to say that there can be no certainty in the
truth of the Protestant religion, because all its *positive*
doctrines are professedly held by Roman Catholics, and
are therefore of divine certainty, according to their own
principles ; while the *negative* doctrines held by Protestants
—that is, the Roman Catholic doctrines rejected by them—
must always be at least uncertain, as being founded on the
peculiar principle of Roman Infallibility. It is said, indeed,
that the divine authority of the Church of Rome is the
foundation of all faith, but this we utterly deny ; God has
not revealed it, and therefore we are not bound to believe
it. It is true that " faith is the gift of God," and " without
faith it is impossible to please God." But faith is believing God—the only proper object of faith is the revealed
Word of God—and it is impossible to derive from it any
article of the Creed which says, " I believe in the infallible
Church of Rome." It is true that the faith is one, and
rests upon one principle of divine authority, but that
authority must rest upon divine revelation, otherwise it is
only a human tradition. The *ultimate* authority on which
all faith must rest is the voice of God, speaking to us
through the *inspired testimony of Christ and His Apostles*—
this is the final resolution of faith on all Christian principles
—and therefore Protestants have surely no less certainty
of faith than Romanists, while they receive that testimony
as coming to them through the medium of God's written
Word, which is admitted on *both* sides, while Romanists
receive it through the medium of their Church, which is
admitted only on *one* side.

The claim to Infallibility may indeed be supported by
plausible and ingenious arguments—a beautiful theory in
speculation, but a dangerous principle in practice. This

will appear more clearly in the practical consequences of the principle, as illustrated in the established doctrines of the Church of Rome. If the Church of Rome be infallible, then all her doctrines must be infallibly true; on the other hand, if any one of these doctrines be false, then the principle of Infallibility must be false, for it necessarily includes all the details which are founded upon its application, and therefore these doctrines may be considered as decisive tests of the Infallibility of the Church.

Let us then briefly consider the peculiar doctrines of the Church of Rome, in the most moderate form, as set forth in the CREED OF POPE PIUS IV. This Creed was published by the highest Ecclesiastical authority as the profession of faith of the Roman Catholic Church at the period of the Reformation, and though it was not proposed to myself at the time of my admission into that communion, yet it is r.iversally received as containing the most authentic summary of the distinguishing doctrines of Romanism. The entire Creed itself consists of two parts—the *first* being the Nicene or Constantinopolitan Creed, adopted by the first two General Councils in 325 and 381, and received by the Church of England; while the *second* part was compiled so lately as the year 1564, shortly after the conclusion of the Council of Trent, and is of course rejected by all Protestants. Here, then, we have the *old* and the *new* Creeds placed in immediate connexion with each other, the *former* received by the Church of England, and *both* received by the Church of Rome. The question is, are the articles of this *latter* Creed to be also received as essential doctrines of Christianity? How are we to decide this question? We must go back to the *beginning*, to the old Gospel of Christ and His Apostles. God has spoken by the Prophet. " Thus saith the Lord, Stand ye in the

ways, and see. and ask for the *old paths*, where is the good
way, and walk therein, and ye shall find rest for your
souls." (Jer. vi. 16.) This is the principle of the
Church of England. It is absurd, then, to charge her
doctrines with *novelty*, since she receives nothing but the
old doctrines of Christianity, as taught in the Bible, and
explained in the Creeds of the ancient Church, while she
rejects all innovations which have since been added to the
Primitive Faith. The first thing, then, that strikes us, is
the novelty of this Creed of Pope Pius IV. It is only 300
years old, though the doctrines of Christianity are 1800
years old, and thus do Romanism and Christianity stand
contrasted with each other, in point of antiquity. The
Church of England appeals to the Holy Scriptures as
the only infallible rule of faith, and she appeals to the
Primitive Church as the only unerring judge of controversy, while the Church of Rome refuses to be tried by
any other spiritual judge but herself. The Church of
England acts on the principle that nothing can be divinely
true which was not held by the Church " from the beginning," and thus she practically adopts the celebrated rule
of St. Vincentius, " to maintain what has been believed
everywhere, always, and by all." The application of these
three tests, universality—antiquity—and consent, with reference to doctrine, is decisive in favor of England and in
opposition to Rome. Every one of the doctrines of the
English Church can be proved to have been held by the
Primitive Church of the first Three Centuries, while not
one of the peculiar doctrines of the Roman Church can be
proved by reference to this authority. This is the very
case provided for by St. Vincentius, as applicable to the
times of the Reformation—" What shall the Catholic Christian do, if some novel contagion attempt to infect with its

plague-spots, not only a portion, but even the *whole Church?* Then he will be careful to keep close to *antiquity,* which is secure from the possibility of being corrupted by new errors." This was the remedy proposed by St. Vincentius—not an adherence to the Pope or the existing Church of Rome, but *an appeal from the present Church to primitive antiquity,* and on this principle the Church of England has acted in her own Reformation. Nor can it be fairly retorted against the Reformed Churches, that they have also introduced new Confessions of Faith for the adoption of their members, for none of them profess to contain any *new articles of faith,* but only to *explain* the Creeds of the Primitive Church, as founded on the Holy Scriptures, and to *protest* against any *addition* to those Creeds. There is no real parallel, in this respect, between the 39 Articles of the Church of England, and the Creed of the Roman Church, as defined by the Council of Trent. The former adheres to the *old faith* of the Catholic Church, and rejects all modern *developments* of that faith, while the latter *defines,* for the first time, some of the most important doctrines, which were unknown to the Primitive Church, and declares them to be *necessary for salvation.* This is the natural consequence of the principle of Infallibility, as leading to *intolerance* in religious principle, and to *persecution* in the exercise of political power. It is said, however, that these *doctrines* are really old, though the *Creed* itself is new. We shall now proceed to this inquiry. Let us examine these articles in detail.

The first of them is as follows :—

1. "*I most firmly admit and embrace the Apostolical and Ecclesiastical Traditions, and the other observances and constitutions of the same Church*" (of Rome).

Here, then, is the fundamental difference between the

Church of Rome and all the Reformed Churches. Both, indeed, profess to receive the Word of God as the only rule of faith. But under this name the Church of Rome includes not only the Holy Scriptures, but various doctrines which are said to have been delivered by the Apostles to the Churches under divine inspiration, though not recorded in their writings in the New Testament. These are called by the name of Apostolical Traditions, or the *unwritten* Word of God. On the other hand, the Church of England maintains (in her 6th Article) that "Holy Scripture containeth all things necessary to salvation; so that whatsoever is not read therein, nor may be proved thereby, is not to be required of any man, that it should be believed as an article of the Faith, or be thought requisite or necessary to salvation. In the name of the holy Scripture we do understand those canonical Books of the Old and New Testament, of whose authority was never any doubt in the Church." This is the very ground of the Protestant religion; and the rejection of Tradition, as an independent rule of faith, was certainly the vital principle of the Reformation. It is true that the word "Tradition" is frequently used in different senses, and this variety of meanings has led to much confusion on both sides. The name is often applied to any *doctrine or practice*, whether written or unwritten, delivered by the Apostles to the Churches, and in this sense all the doctrines of Christianity may be called traditions. It is also applied to the *medium or channel* through which any book or doctrine has been transmitted to us; it is thus nearly equivalent to historical evidence or the testimony of the Fathers, and in this sense it is perfectly true that we receive the Scriptures from the tradition of the Church. It is therefore a mere sophism to say that Scripture itself rests upon Tradition, because this kind of tradition does not relate to any *independent source* of revelation, but simply to the *mode of conveyance* by which Scripture has been handed down to us—and thus, as Bishop Taylor remarks, " this is no part of the Word of God, but the notification, or manner of conveying the Word of God, the instrument of its delivery."[*] But the word is now used by Roman Catholic Divines in a peculiar sense, as the *divine* source of certain doctrines received by the Church of Rome, as distinguished from the Scriptures, yet of equal and independent authority, so that Scripture and Tradition, taken together, are said to constitute the joint rule of faith in that Church. On this subject we may quote the remarks of an eminent theologian of the present day. " The word *tradition*, in ancient writers, was not used in the sense which it has now acquired in modern controversies. The Fathers recommend and venerate the tradition of the Church, in a sense very different indeed from that which Romanists and Protestants now alike use the word, as something distinct from and wholly independent of the Bible—something that must be added to the testimony of Holy Scripture in order to make up the integrity of the Catholic Faith. On the contrary, the tradition spoken of by the Fathers, which was committed to the safe keeping of the Church by the Apostles, which was possessed by the Church alone, and rejected or perverted by heretics, was nothing more than the aggregate of those fundamental articles of the faith which are summed up in the formularies to which we now give the name of Creeds ; the essential doctrines, which were received by all Churches, about which there was no controversy within the Church, and which were, confessedly and without controversy, the funda-

---

[*] Taylor's Dissuasive, p. 214. (Ed. Oxford, 1852.)

46

mental truths, without which no man could be a Christian."*
Now the question is, what authority have we for believing
that *any* doctrines were taught by the Apostles, as articles
of faith, which are *not* contained in their inspired writings?
and the only real answer to this question is founded on the
supposed Infallibility of the Roman Church, which asserts
this principle. How do we know that such doctrines as
the Sacrifice of the Mass, the Seven Sacraments, Purgatory, Invocation of Saints, Veneration of Images, Indulgences, Pope's Supremacy, and other articles of faith, are
essential doctrines of Christianity? They are certainly not
to be found on the surface of Scripture; but we are told
that they were taught by the inspired Apostles of Christ
in their oral instructions, and are therefore divinely true.
But how do we know that they were taught by the Apostles? There is nothing about them in their own writings;
and it is really incredible to suppose that they can be fundamental doctrines of the Gospel, while no allusion to them is
to be found in any one of the 27 parts of the New Testament.
The answer is, because the Infallible Church of Rome has
so declared. There is really no other proof on the subject.
All depends on her Infallibility. Independently of this
claim, then, we are left entirely to historical evidence, and
that evidence is utterly inconclusive in their favor, or
rather, it is conclusive against them. We do not deny
that Christ and His Apostles taught many things which
are not written in the New Testament, but then we have
no means of knowing what they were; we have no
authentic record of any particulars, and therefore we deny
that they can form any part of our rule of faith, because
they are utterly unknown to us. There is no trace of
these unwritten doctrines to be found in the Works of the

Primitive Fathers in the first and purest ages of the Church. The only proof, then, of the existence of these Apostolical Traditions amounts to this, that the writers of *later* ages asserted these doctrines to be taught by the Apostles, after they had been generally received in the Church of Rome, but this evidence comes too late to be of any practical use in deciding the question. There is, then, after all, no real proof of their existence " from the beginning," and thus we are led to the important conclusion, that Holy Scripture is the *only* rule of faith, simply *because there is no other rule in existence*, which can be traced back to the times of the Apostles. We have a strong presumptive proof against the divine origin of these Traditions, derived from the fact, that Holy Scripture, which is admitted to be of inspired authority, appears plainly to assert its own sufficiency; while it never specifies any unwritten Traditions to be added to its own teaching : and this proof is strongly confirmed by the fact, that many of these *unwritten* doctrines are evidently *inconsistent* with the doctrines of the *written* Word of God, whereas both of them must perfectly agree, if they are both equally divine—moreover we have clear historical evidence, which shows that these doctrines are not contained in the writings of the most ancient Fathers of the Church, and were consequently *unknown* to the primitive ages—and further, we have the important testimony of the Fathers themselves, that the Holy Scriptures contain all the revealed doctrines of the Gospel of Christ ; and thus it appears that Tradition itself rejects the authority which has been claimed for it by the modern Church of Rome, and bears witness to the complete sufficiency of the Scriptures. This has been clearly shown by the express testimonies of St. Irenæus, Tertullian, Origen, St. Cyprian, St. Basil, St. Athanasius,

St. Cyril, St. Chrysostom, St. Jerome, St. Augustine, St. Vincentius, and others, whose particular statements may be found in the works of our great Divines on this subject.* It has been said, indeed, that we receive Scripture and Tradition on the *same authority*—the authority of the Church—and that, therefore, Protestants are inconsistent in accepting the one and rejecting the other. But this statement is quite incorrect, if the expression relate to the *modern* Church of Rome. We receive the Canon of Scripture from the *Primitive* and Universal Church, which affords no confirmation of the Roman doctrines of Tradition, as none of those peculiar doctrines which are now held under that name, are to be found in the Universal Traditions of the Primitive Church, which attests the divine Canon of Scripture. Indeed, it has been proved that the great principle of the Sufficiency of Scripture was held by some of the greatest Divines of the Church of Rome in every successive age, up to the period of the Reformation, when the Council of Trent, in the year 1546, introduced a *new rule of faith*, in which Scripture and Tradition were declared to be of *equal* authority.† This Decree, however, was not passed without strong opposition on the part of some of the members of the Council, which was composed altogether only of sixty persons, chiefly Italians, and few of them distinguished for theological learning, yet professing to represent the Universal Church of Christ. On the subject of Tradition, it is recorded by Cardinal Pallavicini himself, the Papal historian of the Council of Trent, that " there were as many opinions as there were tongues," though they finally

* Ussher's Answer to a Jesuit, p. 36. Tillotson's Rule of Faith, Part iv., sect. 2. (Ed. Lond. 1625). Taylor's Dissuasive, p. 184.

† Stillingfleet's Council of Trent Examined. (Gibson's Preservative, Vol. ii. App. p. 110.)

agreed in adopting the same Decree. And thus a new principle was established, which might conveniently be extended to any other articles of faith, in accordance with the rule afterwards laid down by Cardinal Bellarmine, that "when the Church believes anything as a doctrine of faith, which is not in Scripture, then we must judge it to be an Apostolical Tradition." And why? not because it is proved by historical evidence, but because "otherwise the Church must have erred in taking that for matter of faith which was not." Thus we see the connexion between Tradition and Infallibility, the former being entirely supported by the latter; and therefore, when we have once established the great principle of the complete sufficiency of Scripture, we really undermine the foundation of all other doctrines held under the name of Apostolical Traditions, and of the infallibility on which they are supposed to rest. We may well, therefore, adopt the memorable language of Chillingworth, in his statement of this principle—"THE BIBLE, I SAY, THE BIBLE ONLY, IS THE RELIGION OF PROTESTANTS. Whatsoever else they believe besides it, and the plain, irrefragable, indubitable consequences of it, well may they hold it as a matter of opinion : but as matter of faith and religion, neither can they with coherence to their own grounds believe it themselves, nor require the belief of it of others, without most high and most schismatical presumption. I; for my part, after a long and (as I verily believe and hope) impartial search of the true way to eternal happiness, do profess plainly that I cannot find any rest for the sole of my foot, but upon this rock only. I see plainly, and with mine own eyes, that there are Popes against Popes, Councils against Councils, some Fathers against others, the same Fathers against themselves, a consent of Fathers of one age against a consent of

Fathers of another age, the Church of one age against the Church of another age. Traditive interpretations of Scripture are pretended; but there are few or none to be found. No Tradition, but only of Scripture, can derive itself from the fountain, but may be plainly proved, either to have been brought in, in such an age after Christ, or that in such an age it was not in. In a word, there is no sufficient certainty but of Scripture only, for any considering man to build upon."

The next article in the Roman Creed is the following:—

II. *" Also, I admit the Holy Scripture according to that sense which Holy Mother Church has held and does hold, to whom it belongs to judge of the true sense and interpretation of the Holy Scriptures: nor will I ever receive and interpret it but according to the unanimous consent of the Fathers."*

Here we are first to inquire, what is meant by Holy Scripture? It is well known that the Church of Rome includes several books in the Canon of the Old Testament, which are rejected by all Protestants under the name of Apocryphal Writings. The only ground on which they are received by Roman Catholics is the alleged Infallibility of their Church, which has pronounced them " sacred and canonical;" and therefore, if the Roman Church has erred in this definition, her Infallibility must fall to the ground. It is laid down in all standard works of Roman Catholic Theology, that none but that Church, or Apostolic Ministry, instituted by Christ, is infallible in all her decisions; and from this proposition it is immediately inferred that the decision of the Council of Trent, as to the Canon of Scripture, is infallibly true. Thus it is assumed that the Council of Trent is the same with the College of Apostles, and the modern particular Church of Rome with the Primitive Universal Church of Christ, while the space of 1500 years is entirely passed over! Now what are the facts of the case, relative to the question before us? It is certain that these books were not received into the Jewish Canon of Scripture—they were not acknowledged by the Church of God in the time of our Saviour—and therefore they formed no part of the Canon received by Jesus Christ and His Apostles—no passage from them is quoted in any part of the New Testament—nor were they generally admitted by the Christian Church during the first Four Centuries. We are fully justified in rejecting these Books from the Canon of Scripture, on the testimony of the most ancient Fathers and Councils, including the Apostolic Canons and Constitutions—Meli' Bishop of Sardis, in the 2nd century—Origen in the 3rd—Athanasius, Hilary, Cyril of Jerusalem, Epiphanius, Gregory Naz, Jerome, Rufinus, and the Council of Laodicea, in the 4th Century—while the only ancient authorities in favor of the Tridentine Canon are *later* than any of these, consisting of the Council of Carthage, St. Augustine, and the Decrees of Popes Innocent and Gelasius.* It is true that some sentences are quoted from several of them as inspired writings by a few of the early Fathers, who found them in the Latin translation of the Greek Septuagint, in which they were intermingled with the Books of Scripture; but they are not included in the most ancient Catalogues, and are expressly rejected by many of the most learned Fathers of the Church, so that the weight of evidence, even on the ground of historical testimony, is decidedly against their claim to inspiration. Can that Church, then, be infallible, which has pronounced, as an article of faith, the divine

---

* Cosins Canon of Scripture, p. 30. Horne's Introduction, vol. i. p. 497 (Sixth Edition).

inspiration of those books which were regarded as apocryphal by the Primitive Church?

It has been said, indeed, that we receive the Canon of Scripture on the sole authority of the Roman Catholic Church, and that we are also bound to receive its true meaning on the same authority. But this statement is founded on a total confusion of ideas on the subject. We do not receive the Canon of Scripture on the *authority* of *any* Church, but on the *authority* of Almighty God, by whom it was divinely inspired. We receive it, indeed, on the *testimony* of the Church—not of the *Roman* Church, but of the *Universal* Church—not of the *present* Church, but of the *Primitive* Church, which received it from the inspired Apostles of Christ. It has been transmitted to us, indeed, through the *channel* of the Roman Catholic Church; but we are no more bound to accept her *interpretation* of Scripture than we are bound to accept the opinion of a *messenger* who delivers us a letter, as to the true *meaning* of its contents. The Church is the depository of the Oracles of God; but she has no authority, at this remote period from the times of the Apostles, to affix her own meaning as the only infallible interpretation of the text.

But we have here a two-fold rule laid down for the right interpretation of Scripture. The first is in opposition to the right of private judgment, as well as the rights of all other Churches—that it can only be admitted according to the sense of Holy Mother Church. Now it is universally acknowledged in the most comprehensive sense of the words, that " the Church " is the only proper interpreter of Scripture, for certainly no one will maintain that this office belongs to Pagans, Jews, infidels, or heretics. It is not from any of these that we are to ascertain

the true meaning of Scripture, but from Christians themselves, that is, from the Church of Christ, as distinguished
from all other religious bodies in the world. But this
explanation will not satisfy the advocates of the Roman
Creed, who apply this expression to the Church of *Rome.*
It is plain, then, that, according to this rule, Scripture has
no meaning but what the Church of Rome may choose to
assign to it, and she may deduce any of her doctrines from
Scripture, in opposition to its plain meaning, if she is
pleased to declare this to be the true interpretation.
Without her authority we cannot interpret a single text of
Scripture, we cannot prove a single doctrine from Scripture, not even the infallibility of the Church, and the natural
tend ncy of this principle is to set aside Scripture entirely,
and receive only the Church's interpretation of it. But
who gave her the exclusive right of interpreting the
Scriptures for all other Churches and Christians in the
world? The answer is found in the assertion of her claim
to Infallibility and Universal Supremacy. But this assertion rests only upon her own authority, unsupported by
any scriptural evidence, and therefore it must be rejected
as an unwarrantable usurpation. Besides, we may ask,
where is this " sense of the Church" to be found? The
Church of Rome has never given us any authorised interpretation of the Scriptures. The Council of Trent has,
indeed. professed to fix the meaning of a few texts, (viz.
Mal. i. 11. Matt. xxvi. 26, Mark vi. 13, Luke xxii. 19,
John iii. 5, xx. 23, James v. 14,) but in all other cases
we have only the private opinions of certain Divines, which
are not sanctioned by the Church of Rome.

The other rule is, that Scripture is not to be interpreted but
" according to the unanimous consent of the Fathers." Now
this is a very plausible rule in theory, but it is utterly inap-

plicable in practice. There is no such thing in existence as the "unanimous consent of the Fathers," as these ancient writers differed from each other in their expositions of Scripture as widely as modern Divines and Commentators. Indeed, the application of this rule is fatal to the claims of the Church of Rome. For it is a most important fact, that the only points on which the Fathers are *unanimous* are precisely those doctrines of Scripture which are *held by Protestants*, in common with the Church of Rome, while those points on which they *differ* are those traditional opinions which are *rejected by Protestants*, and held only by the Church of Rome. And it is a rule which is notoriously violated in the Church of Rome, as there is no such consent to be found in favor of her own interpretation of particular texts. The practical effect of these rules, then, is to prohibit all attempts to interpret the Scriptures, as few readers of the Bible can be supposed to be sufficiently acquainted with these sources of information, which are thus laid down as the only standards of a correct system of interpretation. It is, therefore, a very natural inference, that, under such circumstances, the study of the Scriptures is altogether superfluous, as their meaning depends entirely on the " sense of the Church," from which all their authority is supposed to be derived; and it is well known that this inference is generally adopted in practice. It cannot be denied, that the private study of the Scriptures, in the vernacular language of each country, is attended with such restrictions and discouragements as to amount to a virtual prohibition. It is not, perhaps, generally known, that, in the Church of Rome, there is no authorised Version of the Scriptures in any modern language, as the only standard text of the Bible is the Latin Vulgate, which, with all its erroneous translations, has been pronounced " authentic " by the Council of Trent, and no appeal is allowed from it to the Hebrew and Greek originals. In all Roman Catholic countries, where the influence of that Church is sufficient, the Bible is a prohibited book, and the study of it absolutely forbidden to the people, unless by a special written permission. Though not directly enjoined by the Council of Trent, yet this condition is required by the 4th Rule of the " Index " appointed by that Council and sanctioned by Pope Pius IV. Every one knows how fully this Rule has been carried out, wherever it is practicable, and how frequently the circulation of the Scriptures has been denounced by the Popes, and the benefits of their study included in the list of " condemned propositions." Does the Church of Rome, then, believe that her own infallibility is taught in the Bible? and does she not betray the insincerity of her professions by her reluctance to submit her own claims to the decision of the Word of God? Does she claim any spiritual power but what is defined in Scripture? If she does, let her produce her authority to prove that she has received some independent commission from above, and we will believe it. But if she does not, why is she unwilling to have her claims examined by Scripture, without first putting her own interpretation upon Scripture? How can she reconcile her own conduct with the declaration of her unchangeable faith and practice? Can there be a single instance produced from the records of ecclesiastical history, during the first 1200 years, in which the laity were prohibited or discouraged from the study of the Scriptures? Here, then, is a complete innovation on the practice of the Primitive Church, on a most important subject, on which the Church of Rome stands directly opposed to the Church of the Fathers. There is no point on which there is a more striking contrast between the ancient Catholic Church and the modern Roman Church, than in their sentiments relating to the Holy Scriptures. The ancient Church regarded the Bible as the only divine source of all saving truth, and exhorted all her members to the constant study of its sacred pages, while the modern Church regards it as utterly incomplete without the aid of her own traditions, and strongly discourages the reading of it by her people. It is in vain to say that this is a mere matter of discipline, as it involves the practice or neglect of one of the most precious privileges of the Christian's daily life, and affects so deeply the growth or decay of the spiritual life in the soul of every child of God; and therefore we must pronounce every attempt to supersede the Bible as "making the Word of God of none effect through the tradition of men."

The next article relates to the Seven Sacraments :—

III. *I profess also that there are truly and properly Seven Sacraments of the new law, instituted by our Lord Jesus Christ, and necessary for the salvation of mankind (although not all for every one)—namely, Baptism, Confirmation, Eucharist, Penance, Extreme Unction, Orders, and Matrimony; and that they confer grace; and that of these Baptism, Confirmation, and Orders cannot be repeated without sacrilege. I also receive and admit the received and approved rites of the Catholic Church in the solemn administration of all the aforesaid Sacraments."*

The Council of Trent has not defined the meaning of a Sacrament, but this defect is supplied in the Roman Catechism. However, there is no essential difference between the Churches of England and Rome as to the definition of a Sacrament, which is understood to be an outward sign, instituted by Christ Himself, for the communication of divine grace to the soul. In this sense the Church of England receives only *Two* Sacraments, while the Church

of Rome pronounces that there are *Seven*, and further declares that they are " necessary for the salvation of mankind (although not all for every one)." Now this exception relates, generally, to Orders and Matrimony; the
others, besides Baptism, being considered, in ordinary
cases, necessary for all who have attained to years of dis-
cretion. Here, then, is a most serious difference, of vital
and fundamental importance, affecting the very terms of
salvation. The only question is, did our Lord Jesus
Christ institute these Seven Sacraments? We know from
the Gospels that he did institute *two* of them, Baptism and
the Eucharist; but of the others we have no account in
Scripture, and no record in the history of the Primitive
Church. It is well known that the name of " Sacraments "
was used with great latitude of signification by ecclesiastical writers, as including all religious rites and ceremonies;
but the first author, who alludes to the number of *Seven*
Sacraments, was Peter Lombard, who lived in the 12th
Century; nor was there any general agreement in the
Church of Rome on this point, as we find, in the following
Century, an eminent Divine of that Church, in a theological
work approved by the Pope, teaching that there were only
four proper Sacraments, two of them appointed by Christ,
and the two others (Penance and Orders) by the Apostles.*
There was certainly no Catholic Tradition for the doctr. ?
of Seven Sacraments, either in the Primitive Church, or in
the Roman Church, down to the Council of Florence, in
the 15th Century, when this number was defined by
authority of Pope Eugenius IV. There are, however,
several texts of the New Testament, which have been supposed to contain some allusion to these Sacraments, though

---

* Gibson's Preservative, vol. II., tit. vii., chap. I.

neither the name nor the thing is to be found in them.
Thus, for Confirmation, we are frequently referred to Acts
viii. 17. But there is here no intimation of any divine institution, nor even of perpetual obligation, as it appears,
both here and in Acts xix. 6, to have referred only to the
miraculous gifts of the Holy Ghost, which was conferred
by imposition of the Apostles' hands. But *there is no imposition of hands* in administering Confirmation in the
Church of Rome, as the *matter* of this Sacrament is pronounced to be Chrism, of which there is no mention in
Scripture; and therefore this passage has no reference to
the modern practice of the Church of Rome. The Church
of England, indeed, retains the rite of Confirmation, accompanied with imposition of hands, as founded on Apostolical practice; though she does not regard it as a
Sacrament, but as an ecclesiastical custom, wisely adapted
to the present state of the Church.

As to Penance, the Council of Trent founds its
divine institution entirely on our Lord's commission to
His Apostles—" Whosesoever sins ye remit, they are
remitted unto them; and whosesoever sins ye retain,
they are retained " (John xx. 23). The Sacrament of
Penance is declared to consist of three parts—contrition, confession, and satisfaction—which are the acts of the penitent;
but there is nothing whatever expressed about the necessity
of faith in Christ and in the merits of His atoning blood.
Yet this Sacrament is pronounced to be necessary to salvation for all who have sinned after Baptism; that is, for
every adult member of the Church. But what connexion
is there between this text and the necessity of *private confession* to a Priest? There is certainly no allusion in it to
the subject of confession, either in its obvious meaning or
by any legitimate inference, as such an interpretation rests

solely on the authority of the Council of Trent, that is, on
the supposed Infallibility of the Church of Rome. And
thus, though there is not a word about confession, directly
or indirectly, yet the Church of Rome, on the principle
stated in the preceding article, declares it to be necessary
to salvation to believe that the practice was divinely instituted by Christ Himself, in this very passage! It does not
appear, however, that the Apostles themselves ever understood the words in this sense, as we never find them claiming
or exercising such a power in the case of individuals. They
declared, indeed, that " God had given to them the ministry of reconciliation," and the great message which they delivered was this, ' that God was in Christ, reconciling the
world unto Himself, not imputing their trespasses unto
them ; and hath committed unto us the word of reconciliation ;" and therefore, as " ambassadors for Christ, they
besought men to be reconciled to God " (2 Cor. v. 18—20).
They knew that God alone can forgive sins, and that all
penitent sinners are freely forgiven through the merits of
Christ's precious blood applied to their souls by faith ; they
reminded their converts of the blessed truth, that " if any
man sin, we have an Advocate with the Father, Jesus
Christ the righteous " (1 John ii. 1) ; but they never exhorted them to come to the " tribunal of penance," to confess their sins to them, and to receive absolution from
them. Nor do we find any trace of this practice in the
Church for several ages after the Apostles. Some passages,
indeed, have been produced from the writings of Irenæus,
Tertullian, Origen, and Cyprian, in support of this view,
but none of them relate to the subject of *private* confession,
as now enjoined by the Church of Rome. We read, indeed, of *public* confession of notorious sins being frequently made to the Church, which was afterwards

gradually superseded by private confession to a Priest, the
first intimation of which, in the Western Church, is to be
found in the time of Pope Leo the Great, in the middle
of the Fifth Century. It appears, indeed, that before this
time, in the Church of Constantinople, there had been a
clergyman appointed to receive confessions in particular
cases; but, owing to some scandal, the office was entirely
abolished in that Church, as well as most other Churches,
in the time of Nectarius, in the end of the Fourth Century; and hence we find St. Chrysostom, his successor in
that See, frequently discouraging the practice of private
confession, and exhorting the people to confess their sins to
God alone.* However, the Roman Church still continued
the practice, though without any rule as to its periodical
recurrence, until at length, in the 4th Lateran Council,
held in the year 1215, it was made compulsory on all the
faithful at least once every year. This rule was further
enforced by the Council of Trent, which now, for the first
time, declared private confession to be of divine institution,
and founded it upon their own interpretation of John xx.
23. Now it is certain that the Apostles themselves had no
power to forgive sins by the arbitrary selection of particular
individuals: they could not forgive any one without repentance and faith, and therefore the promise must be understood in a conditional sense, not in the exercise of absolute,
but of ministerial authority committed to them. But how
can it be proved that this text relates to any but the
Apostles themselves, as there is no reference to their successors in the ministry? or if so, how do we know that it
includes Priests as well as Bishops? And why may it not

* Ussher's Answer to a Jesuit, p. 95. Taylor's Dissuasive, p. 350.
Goodman on Auricular Confession, (Gibson's Preservative, vol. ii., tit. viii.
chap. 1.)

refer to the remission of sins by the preaching of the Gospel, or the right administration of ecclesiastical discipline, or to the Sacrament of Baptism, as interpreted by several of the Fathers? There is nothing whatever in the words, referring to the case of sin after Baptism, nor does it appear that any of the ancient Fathers interpreted this text in the same way as the Council of Trent, and it is certainly very extraordinary that a practice which now forms such a prominent part of the Roman Catholic religion should be entirely omitted in the New Testament, and entirely unknown to the Primitive Church of Christ.

As to Extreme Unction, it is declared by the Council of Trent to be "intimated" by St. Mark (vi. 13), and published by St. James (v. 14, 15). St. Mark says that the Apostles, sent out by our Lord during his life, "anointed with oil many that were sick, and healed them." This was evidently, then, a *miraculous restoration from sickness to health*, and therefore bears a very remote resemblance to Extreme Unction, which is practised chiefly, if not solely, for the *spiritual benefit of the sick and dying*. The passage of St. James seems plausible at first view, but it clearly relates to the same case as that described by St. Mark. The effect of this unction, performed by "the elders of the Church," accompanied with "the prayer of faith," was the recovery of the sick person to the enjoyment of *bodily* health. It has, indeed, been asserted, that the expression of St. James may be interpreted as referring to the health of the *soul* as well as of the body; but this interpretation is utterly inadmissible, and the rules of the Greek language will not allow of any such construction. To "save the sick" and to "raise him up," can mean nothing else than *recovery from sickness to health*, and thus the whole passage must be understood with reference to the *miraculous gifts of healing*.

which were then in the Church. Besides, the modern Sacrament of Extreme Unction seems to have been utterly unknown to the ancient Church. Two or three passages have, indeed, been alleged from some early writers, Origen, St. Chrysostom, and Pope Innocent I. ; but they have been fully shown to have been misunderstood in their application. The truth is, there is not a single clear testimony on this subject which can be produced from any ancient Father or Council of the Church, nor is there any record of the administration of Extreme Unction to the dying members of the Church to be found in all the Lives of the Saints for more than 1000 years after Christ. There was, indeed, first, the Unc. on of the Sick for *miraculous cure*, as performed in early times ; then the practice of anointing all sick persons, with a view to *bodily health*, which is said to have commenced about the Seventh Century ; and finally, the *modern practice* of the Church of Rome, which cannot be traced higher than the Twelfth Century, and was afterwards established at the Councils of Florence and of Trent.*

We come next to Holy Orders. This Sacrament is founded by the Council of Trent on Luke xxii. 19—" This do in remembrance of Me." This is certainly a strange interpretation of our Lord's command to commemorate His dying love by the celebration of the Holy Communion. The Church of Rome has pronounced that by these words our Lord made His Apostles Priests, with power *to offer up the sacrifice of His body and blood.* But surely there is not the slightest intimation of such a view to be found in the text or context of the passage ; nor do these words appear to be restricted to the Apostles alone, but to

---

* Clagett on Extreme Unction, (Gibson's Preservative, vol. ii. tit. vii. chap. 2.)

include all the faithful people of Christ among the laity; and so we find that St. Paul, after repeating them in 1 Cor. xi. 24—26, explains them with reference to all the communicants in the following words—" For as often as ye eat this bread and drink this cup, ye do show the Lord's death till He come." The Apostle thus teaches that the words of our Lord refer to the *communion received by the people, and not to the sacrifice offered by the Priest.* And yet the Church of Rome has pledged her infallibility for the truth of this interpretation, which she supports by anathematising all who dissent from it; while, in accordance with this view, the *matter* of the Sacrament of Orders, in the Ordination of Priests, is held to consist in the delivery of the Chalice and Paten, with a commission " to offer sacrifice to God, and to celebrate Masses for the living and the dead," though this ceremony was not introduced into the Latin Church till the Tenth Century, and is not adopted by any other Church in the world at the present day.* Was this indeed our Saviour's charge to His Apostles, and can that Church be infallible, which has affixed such an interpretation to His words?

The last of the Seven Sacraments is that of Matrimony (Matt. xix. 6). But was not Matrimony instituted by Almighty God from the beginning? Yes; but it is said that it was made a *Sacrament* by Christ Himself. We cannot find, however, that our Saviour ever appointed any *outward sign,* as a channel of grace, to constitute its sacramental character; and therefore, though we recognise its divine institution in Paradise, we cannot acknowledge it as a " Sacrament of the new law." And it is certainly strange, that, with such exalted views of the sanctity of

---

* Burnet on English Ordination, (Gibson's Preservative, vol. 1., tit. 1., chap. 4.)

Marriage, the Church of Rome prohibits her Clergy from
entering into that state, though such a prohibition is expressly contrary to the Scriptures, in which St. Paul
directs that Bishops and Deacons should be " the husbands
of one wife " (1 Tim. iii. 2, 12. Tit. i. 6), as well as contrary to the practice of the Primitive Church f · several
Centuries after the times of the Apostles.*

But further, it is declared that these Sacraments " confer
grace " on those who receive them, and that the free gift
of God is limited to the mere reception of an outward or-
dinance. This is laid down absolutely and without any
qualification, as if all who received them were indiscrimi-
nately partakers of the spiritual grace which they signify.
Indeed, the Council of Trent pronounces an anathema
upon those who say " that the Sacraments of the new law
do not *contain* the grace which they signify, or do not *confer
grace itself* on those who do not put a *bar* " (which tech-
nically means some positive impediment to their effects),
as well as upon those who say that " by the Sacraments of
the new law grace is not conferred *ex opere operato* "
(which refers to the mere act of receiving the Sacraments).
According to this view, then, the Sacraments are to be regarded as *mechanical instruments*, by which their spiritual
effects are invariably produced; so that all who receive
the Sacraments receive also the *grace* of the Sacraments.
This is surely an awful delusion, by which impenitent
sinners are encouraged to deceive themselves with the belief that they are in a state of grace and salvation, while
they are still in an unconverted state, and utterly destitute
of the love of God and the fruits of the Holy Spirit in
their hearts and lives. And yet we find that, in the New

* Wharton on the Celibacy of the Clergy, (Gibson's Preservative, vol. 1.,
tit. i., chap. 5.)

Testament history. Judas Iscariot received the Eucharist
from our blessed Lord Himself, immediately after which
" Satan entered into him," and instigated him to the
dreadful sin of betraying his Master ; while, again, we
read that Simon Magus received Baptism, and was probably
confirmed by St. Peter, though the Apostle declared that
he had " neither part nor lot in this matter," and that
" his heart was not right in the sight of God." There was
surely, no saving grace conferred by the Sacraments in
either of these cases.

The Church of England, indeed, holds that the Two
Sacraments of the Gospel are " effectual signs of grace,
by which God works invisibly in us" (Article xxv.) ;
but she declares that " in such only as *worthily* receive the
same they have a wholesome effect or operation," and that
in every case true repentance and a lively faith are necessary, in order to receive their spiritual benefits. The
Church of Rome teaches that the Seven Sacraments are
the *only channels of grace and salvation,* and that these
Sacraments (Baptism excepted) must be administered by her
own Priests ; and thus the salvation of the sinner is made
virtually dependent on the will of man. These external
instruments are always *interposed* between the sinner and the
Saviour ; his view of the glory of Christ is *obscured* by the
ordinances of the visible Church, by her Sacraments and
her Priests, to whom his immediate attention is directed ;
and while the infinite merits of Christ are believed to be
limited to these particular channels, the practical effect will
be to *substitute* these outward means for the Saviour Himself, in all the freeness of His pardoning grace and love.
For if there is no forgiveness of sins except through the
Sacraments of the Roman Church, what is this but to reject
the sole merits of Christ's atoning blood, and to teach

" another Gospel " instead of the glorious Gospel of Christ ?
The distinguishing doctrine of the Gospel is that of *Salvation
by faith in Christ*; and though this truth is not formally
denied by the Church of Rome, yet it is practically superseded by her system, which teaches the doctrine of *Salvation by the Sacraments of the Church*. But what foundation is there in the Word of God for this exclusive system
of Sacramental grace ? Where is it said that the grace of
God is tied down to the Sacraments of the Church of
Rome ? How different is the language of our blessed
Saviour ! " Come unto Me, all ye that labour and are
heavy laden, and I will give you rest " (Matt. xi. 28) ; " and
him that cometh to Me I will in no wise cast out" (John
vi. 37). This is the blessed truth of the Gospel of Christ,
that " He is able to save them to the uttermost that come
unto God by Him, seeing He ever liveth to make intercession for them " (Heb. vii. 25) ; and that we have " bold-
ness to enter into the holiest by the blood of Jesus " (Heb.
x. 19), without the intervention of any human mediation
whatever, through the prevailing intercession of our Great
High Priest in heaven.

And as to the mode of administering the Sacraments, and performing the other parts of Divine Service in the Church of Rome, we are bound to
protest against the exclusive use of the Latin language,
which is not understood by the people, as " a thing plainly
repugnant to the Word of God and to the custom of the
Primitive Church " (Article xxiv.) We find that St. Paul,
throughout the whole of 1 Cor. xiv., clearly condemns, by
anticipation, such a practice, which is contrary to all the
purposes of religious worship, as it prevents the people
from obtaining any spiritual instruction or edification by
their attendance at the House of God. Indeed, it is sad

to think that there is generally no such thing as united public prayer in the Church of Rome in any known language, the Mass and Vespers being invariably conducted in Latin, while, on some other occasions, a few English prayers are sometimes introduced, the rest being entirely left to the private devotions of individuals. And yet the Church of Rome prohibits the attendance of her members on those services, in which they can join in the worship of God " in spirit and in truth," in their own language. Can that Church, then, be infallible, which teaches a system of Sacramental religion so entirely different from the doctrine of the New Testament an the practice of the primitive Christians?

The next article is the following :—

IV. *" I embrace and receive all and everything which has been defined and declared in the holy Council of Trent, concerning Original Sin, and concerning Justification."*

These two doctrines are of vital importance, as they relate to the cardinal points of our *ruin* by the fall of Adam, and of our *redemption* by the death of Christ. All Christians will admit that there is much important truth contained in these Decrees of the Council of Trent, but there are also some statements which all pious Protestants must regard as contrary to the Scriptures. There is no definition given of the nature of Original Sin—the remedy is described to be the merit of our Lord Jesus Christ—but there is nothing whatever said about the necessity of faith in Christ, as the application of this remedy is limited, both in infants and adults, to the Sacrament of Baptism, by which it is declared that original sin is not only fully forgiven, but entirely eradicated from the very nature of all baptized persons ; and though it is admitted that concupiscence, or the " fuel of sin," still remains in the baptized, yet it is denied that it is truly and properly sin, in opposition to the language of St. Paul—(Romans vii. 7); which is explained by saying, that it is so called because it is "*from* sin and inclines *to* sin." But this distinction opens a wide door for the most dangerous errors as to the nature and extent of sin, and is alike contrary to Scripture and experience.

This Decree does not formally decide the question as to the Immaculate Conception of the Blessed Virgin Mary; but it is well known that it has been recently decided by the Pope in favor of the doctrine, so lately as in the year 1854. Yet it is certain that there is not the slightest trace of this doctrine to be found in the New Testament, and that it was utterly unknown to the Primitive Church, as the first notice of it occurs in the 12th Century, after which some of the most eminent Saints and Divines of the Church of Rome were divided on this question for several ages until its final definition. This instance affords a practical illustration of the progress of "development" in the Roman Church, as we find a new idea, started about 700 years ago, and opposed by some of the greatest theologians of the times, afterwards obtaining a gradual reception, until at length it was pronounced to be a revealed article of the Christian faith. It cannot be denied, then, that the Church of Rome has added a new article of faith to her Creed within the last few years—whether it be called a new *doctrine,* or a new *definition,* it amounts to the same thing. If the definition of the Church makes a thing necessary to salvation which was not necessary before, what is this but a new doctrine? Now it is certain that this power is claimed and practised by the Church of Rome. Indeed, it was one of Luther's propositions condemned by Pope Leo X. that " it is not in the power of the Church or the Pope to constitute articles of faith." It is a plain matter of fact, that Rome requires her members to believe more *since* 1854 than she did *before* that date ; and therefore, her Creed is *not* the same now as it was during the first 1800 years. This is but a single example, within our own times, of the power not only of *declaring*, but *making* new articles of faith, and changing the doctrines of Christianity by these definitions. "To make a *new* thing is easy, but no man can make an *old* thing." How absurd, then, is it to speak of her being the same Church now as at the beginning, when it is perfectly clear that her doctrines are certainly not the same ! And can that Church be unchangeable and infallible, which has introduced a new doctrine, unknown to the Catholic Church in early times ?

The doctrine of Justification was treated by the Council of Trent at great length, in opposition to the views of the Protestant Reformers. No Council had ever pronounced any definition on this subject before ; and besides, as the doctrine of Justification by Faith in Christ was the distinguishing doctrine of the Reformation, the language of the Decree is expressed with great prolixity and with considerable ambiguity. Justification is defined to consist "not only in the forgiveness of sins, but also in sanctification and the renewal of the inner man." The causes of Justification are enumerated under five heads—the *final*—*efficient*—*meritorious*—*instrumental*—and *formal* ; and on the last of these points it is declared that the sole formal cause is " the righteousness of God ;" but then it is explained, "not that by which He Himself is righteous, but that by which He *makes us righteous*." Thus we find that Sanctification is described as a *part* of our Justification, by which the *work of Christ for us* is confounded with the *work of the Spirit in us*—the *objective* truth of Christ *without* us is confounded with the *subjective* truth of Christ *within* us—and Justification itself is declared to be the act of *making* us righteous, and not of *accounting* us righteous before God. This is the foundation of the doctrine of Justification by *inherent* righteousness, or the righteousness of God *infused* in us, as distinguished from the righteousness of Christ *imputed* to us by faith. It seems plainly to follow from this doctrine, that, after all, we are justified by our own holiness, which is called " the righteousness of God," because it is said to be derived from the grace of God in us ; and thus it appears that the ground of our acceptance with God is our own personal righteousness, as the formal cause of Justification, while the merits of Christ, which are admitted to be the meritorious cause, are chiefly employed to give efficacy to human merits. The Council of Trent says—" It is called *our* righteousness, because we are justified through it being *inherent in us*; and at the same time it is the righteousness *of God*, because it is infused into us *by God*, through the merits of Christ." This Justification is admitted to be received " by faith," in such a sense that faith is " the beginning of man's salvation, the foundation and root of all Justification ;" but then it is to be observed that " faith," in Roman Catholic Theology, means a belief in all the doctrines of Christianity, which are identified with the doctrines of the Church of Rome; while it is held that this Justification is conferred through the Sacraments of Baptism and of Penance, and it is further declared that Justification is *increased* by the good works of a justified person, which are meritorious to such a degree as truly to *deserve* everlasting life, as well as an increase of grace here and of glory hereafter.

But how does such a complicated system of Justification agree with the doctrine of the Apostles ? The Council of

Trent, indeed, claims the highest authorities for these definitions. It asserts, as a matter of fact, that this is the doctrine
"which the Sun of Righteousness, Christ Jesus, the
Author and Finisher of our Faith, taught, and the Apostles
delivered." But is this assertion really true? Let us
consult the New Testament, the only authentic source of
information on the subject. We there find that the
Apostles teach us that Justification consists in the forgiveness of sins and the imputation of righteousness without
works (Romans iv. 3—8); they clearly distinguish between
Justification and Sanctification, as essentially distinct in
office, though inseparably connected in practice (Romans iii.
and vi. 1 Cor. vi. 11). They declare that we are "justified
freely by God's grace, through the redemption that is in
Christ Jesus " (Rom. iii. 24); that " Christ is the end of the
law for righteousness to every one that believeth " (Rom.
x. 4); and that ∙ God hath made Him to be sin for us, who
knew no sin ; that we might be made the righteousness of God
in Him " (2 Cor. v. 21). And how was Christ made sin for
us ? Not by our sins being *inherent* in Him, but *imputed*
to Him, when He suffered in our stead. And therefore,
when we are said to be " made the righteousness of God
in Him," this cannot mean that His righteousness is *inherent* in us, but *imputed* to us through His vicarious sacrifice. And thus we find that St. Paul strongly contrasts his
own *inherent* righteousness with the *imputed* righteousness of
Christ, when he declares it to be his earnest desire to " win
Christ, and be found in Him, not having mine own righteousness, which is of the law, but that which is through
the faith of Christ, the righteousness which is of God by
faith " (Phil. iii. 9). The great doctrine taught by the
Apostles was that of Justification by the free grace of God,
through the atoning sacrifice of the Lord Jesus Christ,

applied by faith to every individual sinner who comes to Him : they preached the free forgiveness of sins through the precious blood of Christ, and declared that " by Him all that believe are justified from all things, from which they could not be justified by the law of Moses " (Acts xiii. 39). They taught nothing about inherent justice, or human merit, or the necessity of sacramental confession, penances, and satisfactions ; they extolled the benefits of faith in the blood of Christ, and not of faith in the Church of Rome ; they proclaimed complete redemption by the finished work of Christ on the Cross, fully secured to every believer, in this present life ; they directed the sinner at once to Jesus, the dying Lamb of God, who has made an everlasting atonement for all our sins ; they declared " that a man is justified by faith, without the deeds of the law " (Romans iii. 28), and that " being justified by faith, we have peace with God through our Lord Jesus Christ " (Romans v. 1).

The Gospel of Christ is designed to exalt the Saviour, and to humble the sinner, by ascribing the whole glory of salvation to the merits of Christ alone, and thus it utterly destroys the proud doctrine of meritorious satisfaction for sin, which is so deeply rooted in the natural heart of man. We may well, therefore, conclude with the judicious Hooker—" The righteousness, wherein we must be found, if we will be justified, is *not our own*; therefore we cannot be justified by any *inherent* quality. . . . You see, therefore, that the Church of Rome, in teaching Justification by inherent grace, doth pervert the truth of Christ, and that by the hands of the Apostles we have received otherwise than she teacheth." *

---

* Hooker's Discourse of Justification, p. 38, (Ed. 1618.)

Let us proceed to the next article :—

V. " *I profess, also, that in the Mass there is offered to God a true, proper, and propitiatory Sacrifice for the living and the dead; and that in the most holy Sacrament of the Eucharist there is truly, really, and substantially, the body and blood, together with the soul and divinity of our Lord Jesus Christ; and that there is made a conversion of the whole substance of the bread into the body, and of the whole substance of the wine into the blood; which conversion the Catholic Church calls Transubstan- tiation.*"

We now come to the doctrines of the Mass and Transub- stantiation, which were regarded by the English Reformers as the two greatest corruptions of the Church of Rome. With regard to the Sacrifice of the Mass, it is evident that there is not the slightest foundation for this doctrine in any part of the New Testament, nor is there any allusion whatever to the existence of priests, or sacrifices, under the Christian Dispensation, except in a spiritual sense, in which the terms are applied to all true Christians. But further, it is utterly contrary to the doctrine of the Apostles, as to the absolute perfection of the *One Sacrifice of the death of Christ, once offered on the Cross.* It is the great design of St. Paul's argument, in the Epistle to the Hebrews, to prove that there could be only *one* propitiatory sacrifice for sin, by which all *other* sacrifices were abolished for ever— he shows that the repetition of any sacrifice is a proof of its imperfection; and he dwells, with peculiar emphasis, on the great doctrine, that " Christ was *once* offered to bear the sins of many " (Hebrews ix. 28), and that " by one offering he hath perfected for ever them that are sanc- tified " (Hebrews x. 14). It is said, indeed, that it is the same sacrifice of Christ which is still offered up in the Mass, which derives all its efficacy from the Sacrifice of the Cross—the only difference being, that the one was a *bloody*, and the other an *unbloody* offering, applying to us the benefits of the death of Christ. But all this is totally inconsistent with the doctrine of the inspired Apostle, which entirely excludes, not only the offering of *different* sacrifices, but the *repetition* of the *same* sacrifice under any form. He teaches us, that the sacrifice of Christ can never be repeated, " for this He did *once*, when He offered up Himself" (Hebrews vii. 27) ; that, in order to be *offered*, He must *suffer*, " nor yet that He should offer Himself often —for then must he often have suffered" (Heb. ix. 25, 26) ; and therefore He cannot be offered in the Mass without suffering ; nor can such an offering be an *unbloody* one, because an unbloody sacrifice cannot be a *propitiatory* sacrifice, for " without shedding of blood is no remission " (Hebrews ix. 22). It may be said that this language applies to the Sacrifice of the Cross, and not to the Mass. This is quite true—St. Paul says nothing of the Sacrifice of the Mass ; but every statement of the sacred writer proves that there can be *no other propitiatory sacrifice* but that of the Cross, and therefore that the Sacrifice of the Mass is a human invention, and an awful attempt to introduce another sacrifice, in opposition to the One Atonement for sin. And if it be said, that all this is only a *mystical* sacrifice, in which the death of Christ is commemorated and represented, then we admit that such a view is perfectly consistent with the Scriptures, the Fathers, and the Reformed Churches ; but this is certainly not the view which is held by the Church of Rome. Further, there is no account of any such doctrine to be found in the history of the Primitive Church. Much stress has been laid upon the ancient Liturgies, attributed to some of the Apostles, which seem to favor this doctrine. But it is generally admitted that

these Liturgies have been greatly interpolated, and are
chiefly corruptions of later times, as, indeed, it is well
known that none of the ancient Liturgies were committed
to writing before the 4th or 5th Century. It is true that
the early Fathers applied the name of "sacrifices," in a
spiritual sense, to the Eucharist, as well as to other services
of Christians; and thus the notion of a *proper* sacrifice
was gradually introduced into the Church, and finally established by the Council of Trent. According to this view,
the Sacrament of the Eucharist was supposed to consist of
two parts—a *Sacrifice* as well as a *Communion*; and this
distinction led to the practice of private Masses without a
Communion (and especially when offered up for the deliverance of souls out of Purgatory), which is now universally adopted in the Church of Rome, though contrary to
the New Testament and to the Primitive Church.

The Sacrifice of the Mass is founded upon the doctrine
of Transubstantiation, which forms the other part of this
article. This doctrine rests upon the literal interpretation
of the sacred words of Institution, when our blessed Lord,
at His Last Supper, took bread and wine, and gave them
to His Disciples, declaring—"this is My body—this is My
blood" (Matt. xxvi. 26—28). Now the very connexion
of these words seems to show that they can only be
understood in a *spiritual* or *sacramental* sense. For what
was it which our Lord gave to His Disciples? It was certainly that substance of which he said—"This is My body."
Yet it is evident that the substance which He *gave* them
was the same as that which he *brake*—that which He *brake*
was the same as that which He *blessed*—that which He
blessed was the same as that which he *took*—and that which
He *took* was certainly bread; for it is expressly said that "Jesus
took bread." &c. There is no intimation of any physical

change between each of these successive acts, and therefore, as it was *bread* which He *took* in His hands, so it was
bread which He *gave* His Disciples, when He said, " This
is My body." And in like manner with regard to the
Sacramental c . Besides, we find that our Lord declares
that the *bre* was not only His body, but His *body
given*, or *broken* for them ; and that the cup was not only
His blood, but His *blood shed* for them. Now we know
that His body was not *actually given*, nor His blood *actually
shed*, till the following day. Yet our Lord uses the *present*
tense, and says that His body was *then* given, and His
blood *then* shed for them ; and therefore these words must
be understood as *representing* and *signifying* that great
event which was to be consummated on the Cross. And
if the words are to be interpreted in the *future* tense, (as
they are translated in the Latin Vulgate,) then they dis-
prove the doctrine of the Church of Rome, that our
Lord actually offered up His own body and blood as a
sacrifice to His Eternal Father, at the institution of the
Eucharist, on the day before His Passion. Moreover, we
find that our Lord applies the name of the " fruit of the
vine " to the contents of the Sacramental cup *after consecration* (Matthew xxvi. 29) ; and if it still remained wine
at that time, then the bread, by the same analogy, must
have remained in its former substance. No conclusive
argument, then, can be founded on the words of Institution in favor of Transubstantiation ; and this is candidly
admitted by several eminent Divines of the Church of
Rome, who hold that the doctrine derives its whole force
from the definition of the Church. Indeed, the very same
expression is employed by St. Paul on another subject,
when he says that " the Church is the body of Christ "
(Ephesians i. 22, 23). Now all are agreed that this means

His *mystical* body, and on the same principle we may infer that this expression is to be understood in a mystical sense with reference to the Sacrament; for we find that St. Paul frequently applies the name of "bread" to the Sacramental symbol after consecration, as we read 1 Corinthians x. 16, 17, and xi. 26—28. We may conclude, then, in the words of the 28th Article, that "Transubstantiation (or the change of the substance of bread and wine) cannot be proved by Holy Writ, but is repugnant to the plain words of Scripture, overthroweth the nature of a Sacrament, and hath given occasion to many superstitions." And surely we might expect to have very clear and decisive evidence from Scripture in proof of a doctrine so contrary to all reason and the testimony of the senses, involving such an awfully tremendous mystery as that which requires us to believe that the same body of Christ, which is now in heaven, is also actually present on 10,000 altars on earth at the same moment; and that every particle of the Sacrament, under each kind, is true God and true man, to be adored with all the divine honors which belong to the Creator of heaven and earth; while it was this practice of the Adoration of the Host which formed the principal foundation of the charge of Idolatry against the worship of the Church of Rome, and which, indeed, is the necessary consequence of the doctrine of Transubstantiation.

With regard to the doctrine of the ancient Church, it is indeed quite true that the Fathers used strong expressions on this subject; but they frequently show, by their own explanations—by the comparisons which they employ—and by the arguments which they found upon their doctrine, that their views were very different from those of the modern Church of Rome; while some of them also expressly affirm that the substance of the bread and wine remain after consecration. Thus St. Chrysostom says—" Before the bread is sanctified, we call it bread ; but when the grace of God, by the Priest, has sanctified it, it has no longer the name of bread, but is counted worthy to be called the Lord's Body, *although the nature of bread remains in it.*" * In like manner, Theodoret, speaking o: the consecrated elements in the Eucharist—" After sanctification, the mystical symbols do not depart from their own nature, for *they remain still in their former substance,* and figure, and form, and may be seen and touched just as before." † To the same effect Pope Gelasius—" Certainly the Sacraments of the body and blood of Christ, which we take, are a divine thing, for which reason we become by them partakers of the divine nature, and yet *the substance, or nature of bread and wine, does not cease to be.*" ‡

Such was the doctrine held in the 5th Century, but in the course of the following ages a new system was gradually introduced, ard finally established in the Church of Rome. It is unnecessary to enter more fully into the testimony of the Fathers, and the history of Transubstantiation, which has been so copiously treated by the greatest Divines since the Reformation. It is sufficient to remark that the only authority on which the doctrine rests is the Infallibility of the Church of Rome, which has defined it as an article of faith. This was first done by Pope Innocent III. in the 4th Lateran Council in 1215, though it has been proved that the Canons of that Council were merely Constitutions drawn up by the Pope, and were not proposed for the consideration of the members, nor were they published as the Acts of the Council till the year 1538. This doctrine,

---

* S. Chrysost. ad Cæsarium Epist.—Opp. Tom. III., p. 744, (Ed. Ben.)
† Theodor. Dial.—Opp. Vol. iv. pars 1, (Ed. Halæ, 1772.)
‡ Gelas de Duab. Naturis in Christo (Bibl. Max. Patr Tom. viii.)

however, was fully defined and settled at the Council of
Trent, in the year 1551. It is remarkable, indeed, that
the Canon of the Mass, as used by the Church of Rome
at the present day, affords no support whatever to the
doctrines of Transubst:.... and the Sacrifice of the
Mass, but contains se.... ges plainly inconsistent with
them both; as the sub.... oblation, after consecration, is
described to be, not the .....y and blood of Christ, but the
"holy *bread* of eternal ...., and the chalice of everlasting
salvation;" while the ..... of " the *bread* of heaven " is
afterwards applied to the consecrated Host. The reason of
this is obvious; for the Liturgy of the Mass is itself very
ancient, while the Roman doctrine is comparatively modern;
and hence there is some difficulty felt in accommodating
the old service to the new doctrine.

It is added in the Roman Creed :—

VI. " *I confess, also, that, under one kind only, whole and entire
Christ, and a true Sacrament are received.*"

Of all the practices of the Church of Rome, there is
none which is more directly contrary to Scripture and antiquity than that of Communion under *one* kind only, by
which the laity are deprived of the Sacramental cup. We
find that our blessed Saviour instituted and administered
the Sacrament to His Disciples under *both* kinds, and
charged them to " do this in remembrance of Him," under
both kinds; while there is a particular stress laid upon this
circumstance in one of the Gospels, in which it is expressly
said that " they *all* drank of it " (Mark xiv. 23). It has been
asserted, however, that our Lord made His Disciples *Priests*
by this act, and therefore the *laity* are not bound to receive
the Sacrament under both kinds. But, even if this interpretation were true, it would prove nothing; for the Church
of Rome does not allow the Cup to any of her Priests,

except the officiating clergyman ; and therefore, this is contrary to her own practice. Besides, this argument would prove that the laity are not required to receive the Sacrament at all ; and consequently our Lord does not address His Disciples as Priests, but simply as Communicants. Further, we find that St. Paul, in Cor. xi., gives a particular account of the institution of the Sacrament, and then refers, again and again, to the communion of the people under *both* kinds, as the invariable practice of the Church.

It is a well known fact, and it is fully admitted by the most learned Romanists, that such was the general practice of the Christian Church in all countries for more than 1000 years after Christ ; nor can a single clear instance to the contrary be produced during that period, not excepting the cases of Serapion and of St. Ambrose, which are frequently quoted on this point. It is evident, then, that the Church of Rome, in authorising the custom of half-communion, has acted in opposition to the command of our blessed Lord, the example of the Apostles, and the practice of the whole Church from the beginning. How, then, can this mutilation of the Sacrament be defended? Only on the principle of the Infallibility of the Roman Church, which has thus presumed to alter the divine institution of Christ, on her own authority. This change was first sanctioned by the Council of Constance in 1415, and afterwards by the Council of Trent in 1562, which declares that " Holy Mother Church, acknowledging her own authority in the administration of the Sacraments, although from the beginning of the Christian religion the use of both kinds was not infrequent, yet in process of time that custom being now most widely altered, induced by weighty and just causes, hath approved this custom of communicating under one kind :" after which it pronounces an anathema on those who assert that the

Church was not justified in passing this law. It is **affirmed,** indeed, that the cup—the symbol of our redemption by **the** blood of Christ—does not belong to the *essence* **of the** Sacrament ; but the same statement might be made **with** respect to the bread, and would tend to prove that *neither* kind is necessary for the people ; while this **sacrilegious** practice has been defended by the theory of *concomitance,* which supposes that the very body and blood of Christ, being inseparably connected, are *both* contained under *either* kind alone—an opinion which is founded on the doctrine of Transubstantiation, and both of them of comparatively modern origin. Again, we ask, then, Can that Church be infallible, which has so notoriously erred in depriving the people of the Sacrament of the blood of Christ, in direct opposition to the command of our Lord and the practice of the Catholic Church?

The next article relates to Purgatory :—

VII. " *I constantly hold that there is a Purgatory, and that the souls detained therein are helped by the suffrages of the faithful.*"

There is no definition of Purgatory given here, or in the Decree of the Council of Trent; and there is, perhaps, no subject on which there are such different opinions held by Romanists themselves, as to the *place, mode,* and *duration* of purgatorial sufferings. All are agreed that it is a state of *purification* for those who have departed this life in the grace of God, though not fully prepared for heaven on account of their imperfect sanctification ; it is generally agreed that this purification takes place by means of *suffering,* and further, that this suffering is produced by *fire,* either in a material or in a figurative sense, and that relief may be afforded to the souls in Purgatory by the prayers of the faithful, and especially by the Sacrifice of the Mass. That though the doctrine is thus vaguely laid down, it is well known that it is generally held in a much grosser form, and described in popular instructions nearly in the same language as hell itself, with the sole difference of the *limited* period of its sufferings. Indeed, this view is clearly encouraged in the Roman Catechism (which is certainly an authentic Exposition of the Council of Trent), in which it is declared that " there is a *purgatory fire*, in which the souls of the pious are expiated by being *tormented* for a definite time, that an entrance may be opened for them into the eternal country, into which nothing defiled enters."

Now it is a sufficient refutation of this doctrine, to show that it is *never mentioned* in Scripture—that it is contrary to the doctrine of the Gospel—and that it was *unknown to the Christian Church* during the primitive ages. The only passage of the New Testament which can, with the slightest degree of plausibility, be urged in its favor, is 1 Cor. iii. 13—15, in which St. Paul declares that " every man's work shall be tried by fire," and that there will be some who " shall be saved, *yet so as by fire.*" Now there is scarcely any text which has been so differently interpreted by the Fathers ; and therefore, according to the rule laid down in this Creed, it ought not to be interpreted at all, or alleged as the foundation of any doctrine. Without entering into further particulars, it is sufficient to remark, that St. Paul appears, in the context of the passage, to refer only to *Ministers* of the Gospel, and not to *all* Christians—to the process of *trial*, and not of *purgatorial punishment*—to the trial of their *work*, and not of their *souls*—to the day of the *Lord's appearing*, and not to the *intermediate state* of the soul after death ; and therefore this passage gives no real support to the Roman doctrine of Purgatory. It is contrary to the doctrine of free forgiveness and complete redemption by Christ, and to the happy prospects of believers after death, as taught in the New Testament. It is declared that "the blood of Jesus Christ cleanseth us from *all* sin" (1 John i. 7); and can the fire of Purgatory be necessary to cleanse us from sin? It is the promise of the Gospel—"Their sins and iniquities will I remember *no more*" (Heb. x. 17); and can God remember them still, to punish them after this life in the fire of Purgatory? The death of a believer is described as an entrance into a state of rest and peace in the presence of Christ, till the resurrection of the body; and therefore it is the desire of all true Christians to be "absent from the body, and present with the Lord" (2 Cor. v. 8); while it is declared of the dead in Christ—"Blessed are the dead which die in the Lord from henceforth; yea, saith the Spirit, that they may rest from their labours; and their works do follow them." (Rev. xiv. 13.) There is not the most remote intimation in the Word of God of any further state of purification after death for those who have departed in the faith of Christ, and the peace of God. Doubtless it is true that God visits the sins of His children with temporal punishments in this life, after the remission of the eternal penalty; but where have we the slightest warrant for extending this discipline to the *next life*, by the infliction of Purgatorial torments to be mitigated by means of Masses, Indulgences, and other services, which have laid the foundation of such an extensive mercenary system in the Church of Rome?

But further, such doctrine was entirely unknown to the Primitive Church. It was a very general opinion among the most ancient Fathers, that the souls of departed Christians are not admitted into *heaven itself*, but into a state of *rest in Paradise*, until the resurrection of the body; while several of them also held that all the Saints, without exception, would pass through the purificatory fire of the general conflagration in the day of judgment. Now these opinions, whether true or not, are utterly irreconcileable with the Roman doctrine of Purgatory. If they are true, the doctrine of Purgatory cannot be true ; and if they are not true, the doctrine of Purgatory could not have been generally held by the Christian Church in those early times, when so many orthodox Fathers held an entirely different view. The practice of praying for " the dead in Christ " is certainly very ancient, and may be traced up to the end of the 2nd Century ; but it had no reference to their release from suffering, for the Fathers themselves never mention such an object, and they evidently considered it simply as an act of sympathy and communion with their departed friends, with a special reference to a happy resurrection. Besides, we find from the ancient Liturgies, that they prayed for the souls of the Apostles, Martyrs, and the Blessed Virgin herself, who were certainly never supposed to have been in a state of Purgatory. Moreover, it should be remarked that the prayers for the dead, as used in the Roman Missal at this day, are quite inconsistent with the doctrine of Purgatory ; for they are offered up, as in the language of the Primitive Church, for those who " slumber in the sleep of peace," and for " all that rest in Christ," which is a very different state from that of the modern Roman doctrine of being tormented in the fires of Purgatory. But there is nothing of this doctrine to be found in the Church during the first four Centuries. The celebrated passage of St. Cyprian, in his Epistle to Antonian (often quoted), is admitted by some of the most learned Romanists to have been entirely misunderstood, and it evidently relates to a different matter. No allusion to such a doctrine is to be found in any of the Creeds,

Councils, or Liturgies of the ancient Church. In the beginning of the 5th Century, we find that St. Augustine advanced, with much uncertainty, some speculations on this subject; but the earliest distinct admission of such a doctrine is to be found in the Works of Pope Gregory the Great, in the end of the 6th Century; and after the lapse of many ages it was fully recognised by Pope Eugenius IV. in the Council of Florence in 1439, and finally established in the Council of Trent in 1563. We have good reason, then, to reject a doctrine which is unfounded in Scripture, and unknown to the Christian Church during the first and purest ages.

The next article relates to the Invocation of Saints, and Veneration of Relics :—

VIII. " *Likewise that the Saints, reigning together with Christ, are to be venerated and invocated; and that they offer prayers to God for us; and that their Relics are to be venerated.*"

It is here assumed that the souls of the Saints are now "reigning together with Christ," and " in heaven," according to the Decree of the Council of Trent. The Scriptures, indeed, speak of the reign of the Saints with Christ, but they do not refer it to the separate state of the soul in the heavenly world, but to the future state of the glorified body after the resurrection, in the Millennial kingdom of Christ on earth (Dan. vii. 27. Rev. v. 10, and xx. 4, 6).

Not to insist upon this point, however, the Council of Trent says that " it is good and profitable humbly to invoke the Saints, and to have recourse to their prayers, help, and assistance." This is moderate language; but it is well known that it is far exceeded in practice, and that the Invocation of Saints—especially of the Blessed Virgin —makes up a considerable part of the worship of the Church of Rome, and particularly in the private devotions of her members. It is commonly said, indeed, that they only ask the Saints to pray for them, as Christians ask the prayers of each other on earth. But even if this were so, there is a wide difference between the two cases—the one being founded on personal knowledge, and the other on the possession of a divine prerogative, which makes it an act of religious worship to request their prayers. For how do we know that the Saints hear our prayers, in order to present them before God? If they *do*, is not this virtually ascribing to them the attribute of *omnipresence*, in receiving all the prayers addressed to them in every part of the world at the same time? If they *do not*, is it not entirely useless and superstitious to ask their prayers? We are told, indeed, that this is a mere matter of speculation, and that, if the Saints do not hear us directly, God can reveal our prayers to them, and thus they may become acquainted with our wants, and represent them to God. But surely, if the Saints only know our wants by some revelation from God, it is much better to go directly to God Himself through the intercession of His dear Son; and it is at least superfluous to seek His grace through any other channel. But there is really much more than this included in the doctrine. The very posture of prayer—the practice of *mental*, as well as *vocal* prayer, sanctioned by the Council of Trent—and the petitions expressed in the addresses to the Saints, are such as properly belong to God alone. Even in the public service of the Mass, the general confession of sins is made not only to Almighty God, but also to " the blessed Ever-Virgin Mary, to blessed Michael the Archangel, to blessed John Baptist, to the holy Apostles Peter and Paul, and to all the Saints." Not only the exclusive right of Almighty God to divine worship is deeply injured by this practice, but the exclusive merits of the One Atoning Sacrifice are invaded by the merits of the Saints, which are frequently joined with the merits of our Lord Jesus Christ, as possessed of a similar propitiatory character. It is mere trifling, then, to refer to theoretical distinctions between the different degrees of worship, when the same language, and other accompaniments of prayer, are directed to the creature and to the Creator.

As to the foundation of this practice, the Council of Trent does not venture to make the slightest appeal to the Scriptures, as every one knows that there is not the least authority for it to be found in any part of the Bible. We know that Jesus Christ is the only way to God. He Himself declares that " no man cometh unto the Father, but by Me " (John xiv. 6). " There is One Mediator between God and men, the man Christ Jesus " (1 Tim. ii. 5) ; and therefore we cannot but regard the peculiar devotion which is paid to the Blessed Virgin in the Church of Rome as a dangerous interference with the sole mediation of the Lord Jesus Christ ; while in many instances, and especially as observed at Rome itself and in Roman Catholic countries, it is impossible to defend the practice from partaking of the character of an idolatrous worship, as it really transfers the peculiar honors and titles of our Divine Lord to His Blessed Mother. Is it not strange, that there is not a word in favor of such a practice in all the New Testament, and that the name of Mary is never once mentioned in any one of the inspired Epistles of the holy Apostles of Christ?

It is well known that the Assumption of the Blessed Virgin is one of the principal Feasts of the Church of Rome in the present day. The event commemorated is her supposed Ascension into heaven ; and it is a " pious belief" (though it is not exactly an article of faith) that her body was raised out of the grave a few days after her death, and translated into heaven. But on what authority does this tradition rest? There is no allusion to such an event to be found in any ecclesiastical writer during the first four Centuries. In the beginning of the 5th Century, we have a letter of Sophronius, in which he mentions such a rumor, but states that nothing was known about the facts. Shortly afterwards, we have the account of Juvenal, Archbishop of Jerusalem, who reports the tradition, that the blessed Virgin was buried in Gethsemane, and that her grave having been opened after three days, and found empty, it was concluded that her body had been translated into heaven. There is some doubt, however, about the genuineness of both these Works, and it appears that the earliest author, who undoubtedly mentions the tradition, is John Damascen, who lived in the 8th Century. Such is the evidence in proof of a fact which is said to have occurred 700 years before but which was evidently unknown in the primitive ages. *

But further, there is no foundation for the practice of the Invocation of Saints in Christian Antiquity; there is no trace of it to be found in all the writings of the Primitive Church during the first 300 years after Christ, though in the latter part of the 4th Century we may observe some approximation to it in the rhetorical language of some of the Fathers. But what a contrast is there between the worship of the Church of Rome in the 19th Century, and that of the Catholic and Apostolic Church during the first three Centuries! Can the former be the same Church as the latter? Very remarkable are the words of St. Epi-

---

* Tyler's Worship of the Blessed Mary, pp. 94--114.

phanius, in the 4th age, when opposing the growing tendency
to a superstitious veneration of the blessed Virgin—"Let
Mary be in honor, but let the Father, Son, and Holy Ghost be
worshipped: *let no one worship Mary !*" * How different is
this from the modern practice of the Church of Rome!
And can that Church be infallible, which teaches, under the
pretence of divine authority, a doctrine so contrary to
Scripture and to the Primitive Church of Christ ?

The next subject is the Veneration of Images :—

IX. "*I firmly assert, that the Images of Christ, and of the
Ever-Virgin Mother of God, as well as of the other Saints, are
to be had and retained; and that due honor and veneration are to
be given them.*"

This article is stated in very general terms, as it does
not define the meaning of the "due honor and veneration"
to be given to the Images of Christ and of the Saints. It is,
indeed, a mere abridgment of the Decree of the Council
of Trent, which asserts that the worship is not to be given
to the images *themselves*, and that the honor paid to
them is to be referred to the *prototypes*, or originals, whom
they represent. The Church of Rome teaches that this
worship is not of an *absolute*, but of a *relative*, nature; and
thus she supposes that all danger of idolatry is removed by
distinguishing between *idols* and *images*—the former of which
were adored by the heathen with *divine* honors, while the
latter are to be venerated by Christians with *inferior* homage,
the external marks of which are enumerated by the
Council of Trent, as consisting in "kissing, uncovering the
head, and bowing down before them." Now it is certain
that the same explanation might equally be urged in defence
of Pagan idolatry, in ancient and modern times; as no

---

* S. Epiph. Opp. p. 1064. (Ed. Par. 1622.)

intelligent persons among them profess to worship the wood or stone of which their idols are made, but the deities whom they represent, as the original objects of adoration. This is, indeed, a fearful consideration for professing Christians; though, perhaps, there may be little objectionable in the *practice* of the Church of Rome in these Protestant countries. Still, however, the *principle* is laid down, which is capable of the grossest abuse in those places where the system is carried out to its full extent.

Now, in opposition to this doctrine, it is sufficient to remark that there is not the slightest authority for it in Scripture; and further, that it is expressly contrary to the Commandment of God, and to the practice of the whole Christian Church for many Centuries after Christ. Nothing can be more explicit than the language of Almighty God in the Second Commandment, which is certainly binding on all Christians at the present day—" Thou shalt not make unto thee any graven image, or any likeness of any thing that is in heaven above, or that is in the earth beneath, or that is in the water under the earth; *thou shalt not bow down thyself to them, nor serve them* (Exodus xx. 4, 5). Here we have the most absolute prohibition of the act of making *any visible representation* of any object whatever, *for the purpose of religious worship.* It is objected, indeed, that the word " image " is not in the original, and that the Commandment only forbids the making of *idols*, to be worshipped with *divine* honor. But there is no real foundation for this distinction. The word is of the most *general* meaning, and therefore includes *all images* of every description. It is quite true that it is not the act of *making*, but of *worshipping*, these objects, which is forbidden; and this worship plainly includes every species of religious honor, as exhibited by external acts. We are reminded, indeed, of the two golden Cherubim, and of the brazen serpent, which God commanded Moses to make in the wilderness. (Exod. xxv. 18. Numb. xxi. 8.) But these were certainly not made *for religious worship*, and therefore form no precedent for the practice of the Church of Rome; and accordingly we find that, when the latter was abused to such purposes after the lapse of ages, it was utterly destroyed by the pious king Hezekiah (2 Kings xviii. 4). Indeed, it is well known that the Second Commandment is generally altogether omitted in the popular Catechisms of the Church of Rome, while the Tenth is divided into *two*, to complete the number. It is said, in excuse, that this Commandment is only a *part* of the First, its meaning being included in the former; and that therefore it is unnecessary to insert it at full length, in a mere abridgment of the Decalogue. But we must entirely deny the truth of this statement. The *First* Commandment relates to the *Invisible Object*, and the *Second* to the *visible mode*, of religious worship; and thus they are much more clearly distinct than the Ninth and Tenth (as divided in Roman Catholic Catechisms), both of which forbid the one sin of *covetousness* under different forms. And besides, we find that all the Fathers, with the exception of St. Augustine and Fulgentius, as well as the ancient Jewish Church, differed from the Church of Rome on this point. It is, therefore, at the very least, taking a most unwarrantable liberty with the Word of God, to leave out one of the Ten Commandments under such a pretext.

As to the practice of the Primitive Church, we have the clearest evidence of Ecclesiastical history, that no images or pictures were admitted into Christian Churches for many ages, till they were gradually introduced, as sacred memorials, about the 6th Century, and afterwards approved, and

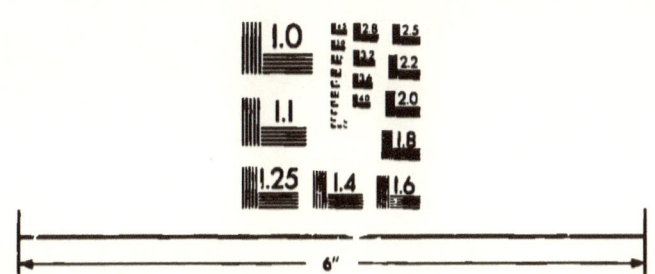

**IMAGE EVALUATION
TEST TARGET (MT-3)**

|← 6" →|

Photographic
Sciences
Corporation

23 WEST MAIN STREET
WEBSTER, N.Y. 14580
(716) 872-4503

... ... worship decreed to them, by the Synod of Greek Bishops, called the Second Council of Nice, in 787. Yet the practice was strongly condemned shortly before, by the Council of Constantinople, in 754, consisting of 338 Bishops, as well as, shortly after, by the Council of Frankfort, in 794, with upwards of 300 Bishops, who rejected the Nicene Council as contrary to Scripture and Tradition; while it was also opposed by many of the most eminent men in the Western Church from the 8th to the 15th Century, till it was finally sanctioned by the Council of Trent. We ask again, Can that Church be infallible, which has decreed, as an article of faith, a doctrine which is so plainly contrary to the Word of God, and to the practice of the Primitive Church?

The following article relates to Indulgences :—

X. "*I affirm, also, that the power of Indulgences was left by Christ in the Church, and that their use is most salutary to Christian people.*"

An Indulgence is generally understood to be the remission of the *temporal* punishment due to sin, in *part* or in *whole,* the latter of which is called a *plenary* Indulgence. Many of them are also "applicable to the souls in Purgatory," and thus these two doctrines are closely connected in the system of the Church of Rome. They are said to have been originally granted in the form of a dispensation from the canonical penance attached to sin, by way of commutation or some other consideration: but the present system of Indulgences cannot be traced farther back than the 11th Century; and the source from which they are supposed to be derived consists of the infinite merits of Christ and His Saints, which form the spiritual treasures of the Church, to be dispensed by the Pope from those "works of supererogation." Indeed, it is fully admitted by Bishop Fisher that

"in the beginning of the primitive Church there was no
use of Indulgences." and that "they began a while after
men trembled at the torments of Purgatory." It is well
known, that the scandalous sale of Indulgences roused the
opposition of Luther against such abuses, and thus formed
the immediate cause of the Reformation. The practice
was defended on the general ground of the powers granted
by Christ to His Apostles, and particularly to St. Peter;
which were understood to belong to their successors, and
especially to the Pope, as visible Head of the Church, and
to extend to the *future* as well as the *present* world. But
it is quite unnecessary to enter into any further refutation
of a doctrine which is founded on such unscriptural principles, and which has led to such dangerous delusions.

The next article relates to the Supremacy of the Pope :—

XI. "*I acknowledge the Holy Catholic and Apostolic Church of
Rome as the mother and mistress of all Churches : and I promise
and swear true obedience to the Roman Pontiff, successor of
blessed Peter, Prince of the Apostles, and the Vicar of Jesus
Christ.*"

This is really the one fundamental article of the Roman
Catholic Church ; for all other doctrines are virtually included in it, as they are founded entirely on its authority.
Such is the Roman development of the old article in the
Apostles' Creed, relating to "the Holy Catholic Church,"
which is thus enlarged, and expanded into all the articles
here mentioned. The *particular Church of Rome* is identified with the *Universal Church of Christ*—which is a con-
tradiction in terms, opposed to Scripture and antiquity ;
the Church of Rome is declared to be "the Mother of all
Churches"—which is utterly false in point of fact; for, beyond all question, this title belongs only to the Church of
Jerusalem, from which all others derived their origin ;

while the Roman Pontiff is styled "the Vicar of Jesus Christ,"—a title which properly belongs only to the Holy Ghost, as our Lord promised to send Him as His representative on earth, and never conferred such an office on any human being. And now, for the first time, after a lapse of 1500 years, the Supremacy of the Roman Church, and of her Bishop, is inserted in the new Creed, as a truth of equal importance with the Trinity, Incarnation, and Atonement; or rather, indeed, of much greater importance, as it is declared by Bellarmine to be the very "sum of Christianity;" while the profession of it is confirmed by an oath of obedience to the Pope.

On what ground, then, are we required to believe this article of the Roman Creed? The only ground is the assumed Infallibility of the Roman Church, which has defined it as an article of faith. Truly it requires a solid foundation to support such an enormous superstructure which has been raised upon it; for it must be observed that the doctrine of Infallibility does not rest upon the Supremacy, but the Supremacy rests upon the Infallibility. It is true that some attempts have been made to prove the Pope's Supremacy on *independent* principles, derived from Scripture and Tradition; but all such attempts have been utterly unsuccessful, as no real support can be obtained from either of these sources. There is certainly not the most remote allusion to the Pope's Supremacy in any part of the New Testament; and it seems impossible to believe that this doctrine can be an essential article of the Christian Faith, while it is thus entirely omitted by every one of the inspired writers. Nothing can be gained by showing that St. Peter held a *certain kind of Primacy* among the other Apostles; because **this distinction belonged to him** *as an Apostle,* and certainly

not *as Bishop of Rome*; for all those instances of such pre-
eminence took place during the early period of his ministry,
and before he had ever left Jerusalem for Rome or any
other foreign place. Now the Pope professes to succeed
St. Peter, not as an *Apostle,* but as *Bishop of Rome,* and
therefore this circumstance proves nothing whatever on the
question of the Pope's Primacy, or Supremacy, as successor
of St. Peter. Besides, it is certain that St. Peter had no
Primacy of jurisdiction over the other Apostles, as they
ll received the same divine commission ; while our Lord
trongly reproves their disputes as to "which of them
hould be greatest," and expressly tells them that "all ye
re brethren ;" and St. Paul declares that "God hath set
a the Church *first Apostles,*" without any reference to
ny official authority of one over the rest ; and he says of
imself that "the care of all the Churches" was committed
o him, and that he was "in nothing behind the very
hiefest Apostles," which is plainly inconsistent with the
upposed Supremacy of St. Peter ; while his own faithful
eproof of that Apostle, at Antioch, shows that he recog-
ised no such Supremacy in him ; and further, we find that
t. Peter himself, in his own Epistles, never assumes the
lightest superiority over his brethren, as he styles himself,
ot the "Prince of the Apostles," but simply "an Apostle
f Jesus Christ," and "an Elder," or "co-presbyter"
ith the other Pastors of the Churches. There is nothing,
hen, in Scripture, in favor of St. Peter's Supremacy, and
till less in favor of the Pope's Supremacy over the whole
hurch.

Independently of Infallibility, then, the whole v. ight
f this claim depends on the true interpretation of our
ord's promise—"Thou art Peter, and upon this rock I
ill build My Church." Now, in order to found an

argument for the Pope's Supremacy on this promise, it will be necessary to prove the following points:—1. That St. Peter *himself* was "this rock" here described. 2. That "the Church of Christ" means the *external visible* Church on earth. 3. That St. Peter was the *first Bishop of Rome*. 4. That this promise refers to him, *as Bishop of Rome*. 5. That, in this capacity, he received supreme authority over the *Universal Church*. 6. That this authority was transmitted to *all his successors in the See of Rome*. It is evident that if *any one link* in this chain of reasoning be broken, the whole argument falls to the ground at once. Now there is considerable doubt about *every one* of these points, and *not one* of them is sufficiently clear to form the basis of an article of faith.

On the *first* point, it may be admitted that "this rock" refers to St. Peter himself. This seems to have been the general interpretation of the primitive Church, though some of the Fathers, as St. Augustine, thought that it might refer *either to Christ, or to St. Peter*[*]; while others, as St. Chrysostom, explained it of St. Peter's *confession of faith*.[†]

On the *second* point, there is no proof that "the Church of Christ," in this general form of expression, is ever employed in the New Testament to signify the whole visible body of professing Christians in the world; and it is certainly more in accordance with the analogy of Scripture language to understand it of the mystical body of Christ's elect members, "which is the blessed company of all faithful people."

On the *third* point, there is really no direct historical proof in the early annals of the Christian Church, and the whole

---

* S. Aug. Opp. Tom. I. p. . (153 Bene.)
† S. Chrys. Opp. Tom. v. p. . (E.J. Bene.)

evidence is utterly inconclusive. The **New Testament** is entirely silent, and the early Fathers are entirely silent on this point. That St. Peter preached the Gospel at Rome, and that he suffered martyrdom at Rome, we have clear historical evidence, though we have no information on this subject in the Scriptures. There is, indeed, the strongest presumption that he could not have visited Rome till a late period of his life (according to Origen and Lactantius, who refer it to the reign of Nero), as the fact is entirely omitted in the Acts of the Apostles, and his name is never mentioned by St. Paul, either in his Epistle *to* the Romans, or in any of his Epistles written *from* Rome, which seems to prove that his arrival there must have been *subsequent* to that of St. Paul. St. Irenæus (who lived in the latter part of the 2nd Century) is the first writer who refers to the origin of the Church of Rome, which he ascribes to the preaching of Peter and Paul; but he expressly adds, that they appointed *Linus* Bishop of Rome*, and we cannot suppose that later historians could have been better informed on the subject, while he evidently knew nothing of the fact of Peter being the first Bishop of Rome, which is indispensable to the Papal system. During the first 300 years, we have only two or three doubtful allusions to this circumstance, and none of them occurs before the 3rd Century. The first is that of an anonymous writer quoted by Eusebius (supposed to be Caius of Rome), who says that "Victor was the 13th Bishop of Rome *after Peter*"†; though this does not necessarily mean that Peter himself was Bishop of Rome, as it might refer to him as the chief *Founder* of that Church. Indeed, it *cannot include* the Apostle himself, because, according to the most ancient Catalogues,

---

* S. Iren. contra Hær. Lib. III. cap. iii. 3. p. 176. (Ed. Ben.)
† Euseb. Hist. Eccles. Lib. V. cap. xxviii.

Victor was the 13th Bishop *after Linus* (inclusive); and therefore, if St. Peter were the first, Victor would be the 14th instead of the 13th. St. Cyprian, also, refers to Rome as the " chair of Peter," and its See as the " place of Peter ;"[*] though he does not expressly assert that Peter was Bishop of Rome, and these expressions might refer to St. Peter's *Apostolical* as well as *Episcopal* office, as the " chair of Peter " is applied by Pope Gregory the Great to the See of *Alexandria*, where St. Peter was certainly never Bishop. In like manner, Firmilian states that Stephen, Bishop of Rome, " claimed to hold the succession of Peter,"[†] though it does not appear how far this claim was valid, and he seems to regard it as an empty boast. This is, I believe, the sum of the evidence of the primitive Church on this point, during the first Three Centuries, though there are upwards of 50 writers of that period, whose Works have come down to us, in part or in whole. There is not one of them who directly asserts that St. Peter was ever Bishop of Rome. When we come to the 4th Century, we find that Eusebius never mentions the circumstance in his Ecclesiastical History, though he states in one place that Linus was the first Bishop of Rome *after Peter*, but he had already stated that Linus was the first Bishop of Rome, " after the martyrdom of Paul and of Peter ;" and he also expressly reckons Clement as 3rd Bishop of Rome, after Linus and Anencletus, thus *excluding* Peter himself[‡]. It is, however, distinctly mentioned in his Chronicle ; but there is no such passage in the original Greek, and it is most probably an interpolation in St. Jerome's Latin translation of that Work[§]. St. Epiphanius, Bishop of Salamis in Cyprus (A.D.

---

[*] S. Cypr. Opp. Tom. I. pp. 120, 153. (Ed. Wirc. 1782.)
[†] Inter S. Cypr. Opp. Tom. I. p 285.
[‡] Euseb. Hist. Eccles. Lib. III. capp. ii. iv. xiii. xv.
[§] Churchman Armed, Vol. II. p. 270.

374) says that *both* Peter and Paul were the first Bishops of Rome.* But the earliest writer, who seems expressly to assign this place to Peter *alone*, is probably St. Optatus, an African Bishop (A.D. 370), who says that " Peter established the Episcopal Chair at Rome, and first sat in it.†" Shortly after this, St. Jerome (A.D.392) states the fact, with all its particulars of 25 years' Episcopate, from the 2nd year of Claudius till the 14th year of Nero‡, which is mentioned by no writer before him. Such was the progress of this tradition, which now began to be gradually received ; but the testimony of these later writers is really of no use to establish a historical fact which is said to have occurred several centuries before, especially as it is inconsistent with the testimony of the earlier writers of the Church. The story of Peter being Bishop of Rome was evidently unknown during the 1st and 2nd Centuries, but in the middle of the 3rd Century, there seems to be some obscure intimation of it, while in the latter end of the 4th Century it is positively asserted for the first time, and afterwards generally adopted as the foundation of the Papal claims. With such evidence, we may justly pronounce the tradition to be merely fabulous.

On the *fourth* point, there is no proof whatever. There is nothing here about St. Peter's connexion with Rome, directly or indirectly. It is impossible to show that our Lord here refers to the Church of Rome. Even granting the first two points, and supposing that some particular locality was intended, the promise may more properly be applied to the foundation of the Church at *Jerusalem*, as it is certain that this was the *first* Christian Church in the world, founded by St. Peter on the day of Pentecost, as recorded in

---

* S. Epiph. Opp. Tom. I. p. 107.
† S. Opt. De Schism. Donat. p. 31. (Ed. Antv. 1702.)
‡ S. Hieron. Opp. Tom. 1. col. 343. (Ed. Par. 1609.)

Acts ii. The very idea of *building* a Church seems
to refer to the *foundation*, and, beyond all doubt,
the Church of Jerusalem was founded long *before*
the Church of Rome. We know also that St. Peter laid
the foundation of the Christian Church among the Gentiles,
by the conversion of Cornelius and his friends at Cæsarea,
as recorded in Acts x. Moreover, it is said that St. Peter
was seven years Bishop of Antioch, *before* he went to
Rome, and why should not this promise belong to him and
his successors in the See of *Antioch*, as well as of Rome?
Besides, it is a most remarkable fact, that not one of the
early Fathers interprets this promise in the same sense as
the modern Church of Rome—that is, with reference to
St. Peter as *the first official representative of a long line of
Episcopal successors.* The earliest writer who quotes the
passage is Tertullian, who explains it as a personal promise given to St. Peter alone, and fulfilled on the day of
Pentecost.* Shortly afterwards it was expounded by Origen,
as applicable, not to Peter alone, but to the other Apostles,
and even, in a mystical sense, to all faithful Christians as
represented by him†. Then Cyprian interprets it as given
to Peter, with reference to the foundation of the Church
and its unity, as typified by one individual‡. These are
the earliest interpretations, and none of these writers explain
it as referring to the See of Rome, or to St. Peter's successors in that See. The same remark applies to St.
Chrysostom and St. Jerome—the two most famous commentators on the Scriptures, the former in the Greek, and
the latter in the Latin Church, at the close of the 4th
Century. In their expositions of this passage, neither of

* Tertull. De Pudicitia. Opp. Tom. IV. p. 432. (Ed. Semler.)
† Orig. in SS. Comment. Tom. I. p. 273. (Ed. Huet.)
‡ Cypr. De Unitate Ecclesiæ. Opp. p. 195. (Ed. Ben.)

them makes the slightest allusion to the Roman interpretation, though St. Jerome was so strongly attached to the Roman See. The testimony of the most ancient Fathers is directly opposed to the claims of the present Church of Rome on this fundamental point of the system. If the Supremacy of the Pope were a revealed doctrine of Christianity, it must have been known to the Primitive Church; and it is utterly incredible that such a doctrine could have been held in those times, when we find that every writer of that period, when commenting on this promise, which forms the foundation of the doctrine, explains it differently from the Roman theologians.

On the *fifth* point, there is no authority here given to St. Peter, as Bishop of Rome, over the Universal Church, as is evident from the preceding remarks. The promise of "the keys of the kingdom of heaven" may well refer to the fact of his having founded the Christian Church on earth, and admitted the first converts, by Baptism, both among the Jews and Gentiles; while the promise of "binding and loosing" was afterwards given to all the Apostles, as well as Peter (Matt. xviii. 18); and thus St. Cyprian asserts that "the rest of the Apostles were the same that Peter was, endowed with an equal fellowship both of honor and of power."

On the *sixth* point, there is not the slightest intimation of the transmission of these promises to the successors of St. Peter in the See of Rome, or in any other capacity. Such a claim seems to have been utterly unknown in the primitive ages. There are only two examples of this kind during the first three Centuries—Victor, and Stephen. The first instance in which the Bishop of Rome attempted any exercise of authority beyond his own Diocese, was that of Victor, near the end of the 2nd Century. He threatened to *excommunicate*—that is, to cease from holding Christian communion with—the Asiatic Bishops, for refusing to conform with him in the time of keeping Easter; but he was dissuaded by the wise counsel of St. Irenæus. Yet he does not appear to have acted by virtue of any authority derived from St. Peter; nor did this act involve any claim to Supremacy, as *every* Bishop had the power of *excommunicating* from his own Church those whom he regarded as unworthy of communion with him. The first Bishop of Rome, who advanced the claim of being St. Peter's successor, was Stephen, in the middle of the 3rd Century, as appears from Firmilian's Letter to St. Cyprian. On the question of the validity of heretical Baptism, he differed from these Prelates, as well as from the great body of the Asiatic and African Bishops, and proceeded to violent measures against them. Yet the attempt was strongly resisted by them, as well as by the Council of Carthage, consisting of 87 Bishops, who treated the language of Stephen with the utmost contempt, and firmly asserted their own independence in the Church of God. There is much light thrown on the subject by the history of this controversy. St. Cyprian may be fairly quoted as a witness, both of the *Primacy* of the See of Rome in point of *rank*, and of the *independence* of all Bishops in point of *authority*. He calls Rome "the *principal* Church," and says that "Rome ought to precede Carthage, *on account of its magnitude*." Yet he writes to the Bishop of Rome on terms of *perfect equality*, and addresses him as his "brother" and "colleague;" while he maintains that "there is one Episcopacy, part of which is held by every Bishop with full authority;" and again, he thus addresses the Bishops at the Council of Carthage, in opposition to **Pope** Stephen—"None of us constitutes himself a Bishop **of**

Bishops, or forces his colleagues to a necessity of obeying him by a tyrannical terror, since every Bishop has full power to determine for himself, and can no more be judged by others than he can judge them."[*] And further, he denounces the Pope as "a friend of heretics, and an enemy of Christians." It is evident that St. Cyprian did not regard the See of Rome as the divinely appointed, centre of unity, and her Bishop as the infallible Judge of controversy. Firmilian writes still more strongly, and complains of the "open and manifest folly of Stephen," and of his "dissension with so many Bishops throughout the whole world," while he plainly tells the Pope that he was "worse than all heretics," and thus addresses him— "What a great sin you have heaped on yourself, when you have cut off yourself from so many flocks! For you have cut *yourself* off. Do not deceive yourself. Since *he* is truly the schismatic, who makes himself an apostate from the communion of ecclesiastical unity; for while you think that all are excluded from *you*, you have only excluded *yourself* from all."[†] These ancient Bishops, then, regarded the Pope as guilty of schism by his intolerant conduct; and they certainly did not think that communion with the Church of Rome was necessary to communion with the Catholic Church. Nor is there any evidence to be produced on the other side, in order to prove that these Prelates were singular in their opinions, or that their conduct was viewed with disapprobation by their brethren, in their opposition to the Bishop of Rome.

In the following Century, we find the first steps towards the Supremacy laid by the Council of Sardica, in 347, which gave the Bishop of Rome a species of appellate

* S. Cypr. Opp. p. 329.
† Inter S. Cypr. Opp. p. 150.

jurisdiction, " in honor of St. Peter's memory ;" while, some years later, St. Jerome addresses Pope Damasus, as holding the See of Peter, " the rock on which the Church was built ;" and in the 5th Century, we find this doctrine more fully developed in the language of three Popes—Boniface I., Leo I., and Gelasius I., as well as in the proceedings of the General Councils of Ephesus and Chalcedon, in 431 and 451 ; after which we meet with frequent contests for the Supremacy between the Bishops of Rome and of Constantinople, carried on for several Centuries, until the former eventually gained the victory over his rival.

Various causes, indeed, contributed to the gradual encroachments of the Bishop of Rome upon the rights of other Bishops. Some of these were of a temporal, and others of a spiritual nature, while both were employed, by a combination of favorable circumstances, to promote the designs of ecclesiastical ambition. The great importance of Rome as the Imperial City—the removal of the Court to Constantinople and to Ravenna—the Pope's position as Patriarch of the West—the Apostolical origin of that Church—the Edicts of Emperors—the Fall of the Roman Empire in the West—the donations of Christian Princes—the general ignorance of the times—these and other events tended to give the See of Rome such a pre-eminence over other Churches, as to prepare the way for the claim of universal Supremacy, founded on divine right, and derived from the succession of Peter. There can be no doubt, indeed, that, in early times, all other Churches were in *communion* with the Church of Rome ; and further, that a certain *primacy of order* was conceded to the Bishop of Rome among other Bishops, as a matter of ecclesiastical arrangement ; but this was totally distinct from that absolute *subjection* to the Roman Pontiff, which was afterwards claimed as a matter of *divine right*; and besides, it must be remembered that the circumstances of the case were entirely different, as the Church of Rome was then a pure branch of the Catholic Church, whereas she has since introduced a new Creed of strange doctrines, which she has imposed as the only condition of communion with her.

We conclude, then, that the Supremacy of the Pope was an act of *usurpation* over the rights of all other Christian Churches, alike contrary to Scripture and to primitive antiquity, while it involves the grossest corruptions of Christian doctrine ; and we ask again, Can that Church be infallible, which has defined this point as an essential article of the Christian faith?

The last article of the Roman Creed is as follows :—

XII. " *Likewise all other things delivered, defined, and declared by the sacred Canons, and Œcumenical Councils, and especially by the Holy Council of Trent, I unhesitatingly receive and profess ; and at the same time, all things contrary, and heresies whatsoever condemned, and rejected, and anathematised by the Church, I likewise condemn, reject, and anathematise.*"

This is a most comprehensive declaration, including a vast body of theological definitions, with which few persons can be acquainted, and which is simply resolved into the profession of unqualified submission to the Church of Rome. It is generally stated that there are Eighteen Councils called Œcumenical, or Universal, as representing the *whole Church on earth* ; though it is evident that, properly speaking, there never was such a Council, as the Clergy and Laity were not represented in those assemblies (contrary to the proceedings of the Council of Jerusalem, Acts xv. 22, 23), while the Bishops comprising them have always been **a** *small minority*, and yet their Decrees are considered binding on the absent members and on the whole Church. Especially since the separation between the Eastern and Western Churches, these Councils can have no just claim to the title of Œcumenical, as they were entirely composed of members of the latter body. The first of these was the Lateran Council in 1123, and the last the Trent Council in 1545-63. This is, indeed, the most important of them all, as it related particularly to the controversies of the Reformation, and therefore it is especially named in this article. The Reformers, indeed, had always professed their readiness to submit their cause to a free and legitimate Council of the Universal Church, whose decisions should be founded on the Holy Scriptures. But the Council of Trent was neither *free* nor *general*, and therefore it was utterly incompetent to effect the purposes for which it was convened. It was summoned by the Pope himself, who presided in it by his Legates, and thus the accused party was sole judge in his own cause. It was not *free*, for its members were all adherents of the Church of Rome, bound by oath to maintain the interests of the Pope, while nothing was allowed to be debated, except under the direction of the Legates, who received their instructions from Rome. It was surely impossible to obtain an impartial decision from such a Council. And it was not *general*, for it excluded all representatives from the Greek and Eastern Churches, as well as from the Reformed Churches, being chiefly composed of Italian Bishops, whose number was more than twice as great as that of all other countries put together. It is absurd to regard such a meeting as an Œcumenical Council, representing the Universal Church. Instead of healing the wounds of the Church, it only rendered them more incurable by its new doctrines and definitions, including a multitude of opinions, which had been hitherto held as open questions, or probable conjectures, while these were now fixed as articles of faith, not on the ground of Scripture only, but also of the unwritten Traditions sanctioned by authority of the Council. The cause of the Reformation was prejudged at Rome, and condemned at Trent. It is in vain to speak of the authority of the Church on these questions, for " the Church" really means the Pope; and thus the effect of the Roman system is to bind the consciences of all Christians into absolute obedience to the will of one man, who claims the right to govern the Universal Church of God with a divine commission.

I have thus taken a brief review of the distinguishing doctrines of the Church of Rome, in connexion with her exclusive pretensions to Divine Infallibility, and I have endeavored to show that these doctrines have no real foundation in the Word of God, as interpreted by the Primitive Church. It thus appears, as Bishop Taylor says, that " they are indeed new, and brought into the Church, first by way of opinion, and afterwards by power, and at last, by their own authority, decreed into laws and articles." We appeal to Scripture and to the purest antiquity, but we find none of these doctrines in the Church during the first three Centuries, though we admit that the elements, or germs, of several of them may be discovered before the close of the 4th Century; and therefore, whatever claims some of them may have to a comparative antiquity, they must be regarded as religious innovations, or corruptions of the Christian Faith. It follows, then, that the Church of Rome, which teaches them as essential parts of the faith, *has erred in point of fact*, and consequently, that she is *not infallible*. She teaches doctrines which were never revealed by Almighty God, and therefore she has no claim to any divine authority. All the supposed proofs of her Infallibility rest upon abstract probabilities, or arbitrary interpretations, which vanish before the light of Scriptural evidence brought to bear upon her doctrines and practices; and thus the proofs of her *fallibility* are much stronger than the proofs of her *infallibility*, as the former rest upon positive *facts*, and the latter upon abstract *theories*. And, in the preceding remarks, I have attempted to explain, for the benefit of others, how I was led *into* the Church of Rome by the supposed proofs of her *Infallibility*, and how I was led *out of* that Church by the convincing proofs that she had *actually erred* in matters of faith. It is, indeed, a remarkable contrast between the articles of the *old* and the *new* Creeds, that the former tend to promote the glory of *God*, and the latter the glory of *man*. There is nothing in the Roman Creed which has any tendency to exalt the Lord Jesus Christ as the only Saviour of sinners, or to honor the Holy Spirit as the only Author of all sanctifying grace : while every article tends to exalt the Pope and Priesthood of the Church of Rome, in their spiritual dignity, as invested with the mysterious power of performing the miracle of Transubstantiation, offering up the Sacrifice of the Mass for the living and the dead, forgiving sins, and dispensing the Sacraments for the salvation of men. This is surely a very suspicious circumstance in itself, independently of any direct evidence against them.

Perhaps the most plausible argument in favor of the Roman doctrines is founded on the historical difficulty of accounting for their origin and progress in the Church. These doctrines, it is said, were generally held in the Latin Church for many ages *before* the Reformation, and therefore we are bound to believe that they were *always* in the Church, unless we can fix the precise *time and place* of their introduction. This objection, however, is of little weight in opposition to contrary evidence. If these doctrines are really contrary to the Word of God, this is quite a sufficient proof that they must be human inventions, and it is little more than a matter of curious research to inquire into the historical circumstances relating to their rise and growth in the Church. If they are not in the Bible, this is enough for all practical purposes, as the question does not relate to the *time* of their invention, but to the *fact* of their human origin. We have, however, a *negative* proof founded on the silence of the early Fathers, which shows that they were not held by the Primitive Church, as these ancient writings contain no allusion to such doctrines, entirely omit them in their Creeds and confessions of faith, and include statements of doctrine which are utterly inconsistent with the Roman Creed.

It may be said, indeed, that the *Scriptures* are apparently in favor of Protestantism, but the *Fathers* are in favor of Romanism. If this be true, then it is certain that the *former* must be adopted in preference to the *latter*, as the Scriptures were the first inspired records of Christianity, while the writings of the Fathers are only the later, uninspired, commentaries of fallible men. But the statement is not true with reference to the *most ancient* Fathers, whose Works strongly confirm the Scriptural simplicity of Protestant doctrine; and why should the testimony of the *present Church of Rome* be preferred to that of the *Primitive Church of Christ?* There is, indeed, a serious historical difficulty to be removed on *each* side. If Romanism be *true*, how is it that its doctrines are not to be found in the *earliest* ages? and if it be *not* true, how is it that these doctrines generally prevailed in the *later ages?* It may be said that the Protestant theory of the gradual corruption of Christianity is only an hypothesis. True; but it is an hypothesis *supported by facts*, while the Roman theory of the universal reception of its peculiar doctrines in all ages of the Church from the beginning is also an hypothesis, but totally *unsupported* by historical evidence.

It is unreasonable, then, to demand a direct proof of the novelty of these doctrines, when their progress was of such gradual development, when so few historical notices relating to these facts have come down to our times, and when there is the same difficulty about the exact date of other changes, which are universally admitted to be innovations on the ancient practice. Every one knows, for instance, that the languages of modern Europe are quite different from those spoken in the days of the Apostles—they must have been gradually changed from their original form; and yet it is impossible to fix the exact period when the change took place. In like manner, all admit that the Holy Communion was administered under both kinds for many ages after the Apostles, and that for several centuries past the cup has been taken away from the laity : here is a public and visible change, and yet who can tell at what precise time this change took place? We cannot wonder, then, that there is some obscurity about the exact date of the corruption of particular doctrines and practices on other points, which were not so palpable to common observation.

Still, however, after all, we have sufficiently clear and positive evidence on several of these innovations. Let us look at a few historical facts relating to the origin of these doctrines. The latest of these is the Immaculate Conception, defined in 1854, contrary to the belief of the ancient Church. Again, the Rule of Faith itself, which makes Tradition equal to Scripture, was first established by the

ruption
it is an
icory of
all ages
iothesis,

of of the
of such
tices re-
nes, and
; date of
be inno-
s, for in-
re quite
ostles—
original
id when
that the
inds for
nturies
iere is a
hat pre-
er, then,
the cor-
points,

car and
Let us
f these
Joncep-
ancient
makes
by the

Council of Trent in 1546. The doctrines of Purgatory and Seven Sacraments were not defined till the Council of Florence in 1439. Communion under one kind (however uncertain in its origin) was authorised by the Council of Constance in 1415. The prohibition of the Scriptures to the laity was first sanctioned by the Council of Toulouse in 1229. Transubstantiation and annual Confession were introduced by the 4th Lateran Council in 1215. The worship of Images by the Second Council of Nice in 787. The Service in the Latin tongue, indeed, underwent no essential change in the Church of Rome, but the *language itself* did; and thus, while the strict *letter* was observed, a new *principle* was adopted in the worship of God. How, then, can it be said, that, with all these innovations, the Church of Rome is the same as she was from the beginning, although she may have constantly preserved her external unity in visible succession?

The strongest prejudice against the doctrines of the Reformation, in the minds of Romanists, is that of their supposed novelty; and yet this charge is quite unreasonable, when its design was to restore the old doctrines of Christianity to their primitive state; and the only way in which this charge can be proved is by showing that its doctrines are different from those taught by Christ and His Apostles, as contained in the New Testament, which is the only certain standard of primitive antiquity. The question, which is the *old* religion, and which is the *new?* Now the old religion is evidently that which holds the *old doctrines* of Christianity, even though the Church which teaches these doctrines may have been newly constructed in modern times; and therefore it is not enough to show that the *new doctrines* were held long before the Reformation, but it must be shown that they are the original doctrines of Christianity, held by the Primitive Church. We have, therefore, several answers to the question, " Where was the Protestant religion before the Reformation?" It may, indeed, be fairly retorted, " Where was the Roman Catholic religion before the Council of Trent?" for it certainly existed in a very unfinished state before that Council. But, with reference to the question before us, we may reply, the Protestant religion was contained *in the Bible*, in which the doctrines of the Gospel were deposited by the Apostles and Prophets, and in which none of the peculiar doctrines of the Roman Church are to be found. It may be said that the Apostles left their doctrines with the Church. So, indeed, they did. But we deny that the modern Church of Rome is the same with the primitive Church of Christ; while it cannot be denied that the Bible is the same now as in the days of the Apostles. Further, we answer, that our religion is to be found *in the Primitive Church*, in the first and best ages of Christianity, as recorded in the Works of the early Fathers; and we are quite willing to be tried by this standard. It is true that the name of Protestantism did not exist at that time. But this name signifies merely a " protest " against the *errors* of Romanism, and these errors were not in existence at the time. So far, then, we have both scriptural and historical Christianity in favor of Protestantism. But we have another answer. Our religion may be found *just where it was before the Reformation*. We may consistently admit that the Church of Christ was always visible, even in the darkest ages, not only in the various bodies of Christians who successively existed in those times, separate from Rome, and who adhered to the doctrines of the Bible, but even *in the Church of Rome itself*, which we acknowledge to be a *true* Church, though we deny her to be a *pure* Church.

For the Reformation did not consist in founding a *new re-ligion* or a new Church, but in *purifying* the existing sys-tem from its *corruptions*, by rejecting those innovations which had been added to the faith in later times. We have no infallible assurance that the great body of the outward visible Church would always continue in the public profession of the pure religion of the Gospel ; and yet this supposition forms the ground of one of the strongest objections that can be urged against the Reform-ation. But, after all, there is no promise of Christ to that effect, and it is contrary to the whole analogy of the Jewish Church, so that we have no reason to expect it under the Christian Dispensation. Besides, we have a special warning on this subject, addressed to the Church of Rome by the Apostle Paul, who refers to this very analogy, and thus admonishes that Church—"Thou standest by faith ; *be not high minded, but fear :* for if God spared not the natural branches, take heed lest He also spare not thee" (Romans xi. 20, 21.) There is no promise of any exemption from apostacy here given to the Roman Church; but, on the contrary, we find that she, above all others, is threatened with total rejection in the event of her unfaithfulness, as the Apostle states the alternative—"goodness, if thou continue in His goodness ; otherwise *thou also shalt be cut off,*" as the "natural branches," the Jews, "were broken off because of unbelief." We have no right to assume, then, that the Church of Rome, or any other Church, would always be infallibly preserved from error and apostacy ; or that the true religion of Christ, free from all human corruption, would always be main-tained by the visible Church in every age. And yet it ap-pears that this assumption was the first motive assigned by Chillingworth for renouncing Protestantism—"Because per-

petual visible profession, which could never be wanting to
the religion of Christ, or any part of it, is apparently
wanting to Protestant religion, so far as concerns the points
in contestation." And, after leaving the Church of Rome,
he answers his own objection thus—" God hath neither
decreed nor foretold, that His true doctrine should, *de facto*,
be always visibly professed, without any mixture of false-
hood."

But further, it must be remembered that, according to
the interpretation of the most eminent Protestant Divines,
God *has* " decreed and foretold " the very *reverse*—namely,
that there should be a great Apostacy, or corruption of
pure Christianity, within the visible Church of Christ;
which, in their opinion, has been exactly fulfilled in the
Church of Rome; and this circumstance completely re-
moves all supposed difficulty on the subject. It is well
known that this view of Prophecy was almost universally
held by the Reformers of the 16tth Century; and that it
was one of the principal grounds on which they maintained
the duty and necessity of abandoning the Roman Communion, as an Apostate Church. It was generally believed
that the Church of Rome was " the Apostacy " predicted
by St. Paul in 2 Thess. ii. 3—" the Apostacy of the latter
times," foretold by the same Apostle in 1 Tim. iv. 1—3—
as well as the " Babylon " of the Apocalypse, described by
St. John, in Rev. xvii. xviii. Nay, more, it was held that
the Pope of Rome was the " little horn " of Dan. vii—
" the man of sin, the son of perdition, the wicked one " of
2 Thess. ii. 3—10—" the Antichrist " of St. John,
1 John ii. 18—and finally, " the Beast " of Rev. xiii. 1—8.

I do not propose to enter into a detailed examination of
these Prophecies, but I must make a few observations on
one of them, as it has produced a deep impression on my

own mind. It appears to me, then, that there is the strongest evidence in support of the application of the Apocalyptic Vision of Babylon to the Church of Rome. In the first place, it is certain that the name of "Babylon," in that prediction, refers to Rome; and this is generally held by all Expositors, of the Roman as well as Reformed Churches. Indeed, it seems impossible to apply it to any other locality on the face of the earth, as it is expressly interpreted that "the seven heads are *seven mountains*" (Rev. xvii. 9), which every classical reader knows to be a proverbial description of Rome, according to its geographical situation, as stated by Pagan writers. And again, "the woman which thou sawest is *that great city*, which reigneth over the kings of the earth" (Rev. xvii. 18); which was precisely the political position of Rome at the time when this Prophecy was written. Now the principal event foretold in this Vision is the Fall of Babylon. But this event is yet *future*. This is evident, because Babylon, or Rome, is not yet destroyed. It is predicted that "the ten horns," or kings, "*shall burn her with fire*" (Rev. xvii. 16). And moreover, the Fall of Babylon is immediately connected with the "Marriage of the Lamb," and the Second Advent of Christ from heaven (Rev. xix.) This description, therefore, cannot apply to the ruin of *Pagan* Rome, or the Fall of the Roman Empire; for these events have taken place long since, and yet Rome is still in existence.

Roman Catholic Expositors differ in their interpretation of the Fall of Babylon, some regarding it as *past*, others as *future*. According to Bossuet, this prophecy was fulfilled by the capture of Rome by Alaric, King of the Goths, in the year 410. But if so, what is the consequence? "Babylon the great is fallen, is fallen, and is *become the habitation of Devils*, and the hold of every foul spirit"

(Rev. xviii. 2). Will any Roman Divine admit that, since that event—that is, during the whole period of the Papacy—Rome "is become the habitation of devils," and that she is *fallen to rise no more*, according to the prediction? (Rev. xviii. 21.) On that interpretation, it is impossible to avoid this inference; and yet such an admission would be fatal to their own system, as well as contrary to the facts of history. But, according to Bellarmine and others, the fulfilment of this prophecy is yet *future*. They hold that Rome is again to become a *Pagan* city, to persecute the Church, and to be destroyed by Antichrist. But this is a mere hypothesis, invented to get rid of the Protestant application to *Papal* Rome. On each of these two systems, then, Rome *Pagan* is the sole subject of the prophecy— according to the one, commencing with Idolatry, and according to the other, apostatising into Idolatry; and as for Rome *Christian*, between these two states, it is distinctly confessed by Bossuet, that "there is not the least trace of the Church of Rome to be found in the Apocalypse." Now it is certainly strange that, if Rome be the subject of the prophecy, there is not the slightest allusion to it as the head of the Christian Church; and that an inspired book, which is supposed to reveal the future history of the Church, should be totally silent about the "mother and mistress of all Churches." But, indeed, there is such a continu... scription in the whole prophecy, as leave no room for such a *transition* from Paganism to Christianity and then from Christianity to Paganism. Rome is not des cribed as existing in two or more successive states; she i Babylon from beginning to end. Can it be possible, ther that Christ has conferred a spiritual Supremacy upon Church established in a city which He has uniforml taught us to regard as "Babylon."—"the land of grave images " ? Is it credible that Babylon—the enemy of Jerusalem—is herself really the spiritual Jerusalem—" the holy city "—" the place which the Lord hath chosen " as the centre of His Church on earth? that while the mystical *name* is suggestive of *Idolatry*, the *place* itself should be the source and seat of true *Christianity ?*

But there is one important circumstance, which destroys, at once, both these interpretations of the prophecy. We find that Babylon is mystically described as "the Great *Harlot*," and her sin is that of spiritual fornication with the kings and inhabitants of the earth (Rev. xvii. 1, 2). Now this is an emblem which is frequently employed in the Old Testament, to denote, not the sin of *Pagan Idolatry*, but the *corruption of the true religion*, and the introduction of idolatrous practices into the visible Church of God among the Jewish people ; and therefore, when it is employed in the New Testament, it must relate to a corresponding sin in the visible Christian Church. "Babylon," therefore, means not only a *city*, but a professing *Church*, or religious system, and Rome as the head of that Church ; and consequently it cannot refer to Rome *Pagan*, either past or *future*, but to Rome *Papal*, or a corrupt Christian Church ; while the "many waters" on which she sits &c. explained as denoting " peoples, and multitudes, and nations, and tongues" (Rev. xvii. 15), or the principal kingdoms of modern Europe, which have submitted to the Papacy. Again, we find that Babylon is described as a *persecuting* power—"I saw the woman drunken with the *blood of the Saints*, and with the blood of the martyrs of Jesus " (Rev. xvii. 6). " And in her was found the *blood of Prophets*, and of Saints, and of all that were slain upon the earth " (Rev. xviii. 24). It is this which explains the circumstance of St. John " wondering with great admiration," as there was nothing remarkable in the persecution of the Saints by a *Pagan* power, while such a practice on the part of a professing *Christian* Church must justly excite the greatest astonishment. Further, she is described as "arrayed in *purple, and scarlet color*" (Rev. xvii. 4), which so exactly applies to the splendor of the ecclesiastical vestments in the Church of Rome, to which these colors are peculiar, as no other Church has adopted them; while a striking contrast is drawn between her character as an Apostate Church, under the name of "the great *Harlot*," and that of the true mystical Church of Christ, as the "*Bride* of the Lamb" of God (Rev. xix. 2, 7).

All these circumstances, then, agree in their application to the Church of Rome, while they cannot be applied to any other religious system that has ever existed in the world. And accordingly, we are told of a warning "voice from heaven," addressed to God's people in Babylon— "*Come out of her, My people*, that ye be not partakers of her sins, and that ye receive not of her plagues" (Rev. xviii. 4). We learn from this solemn admonition, that God has an elect people, who are still in Babylon, or the Church of Rome; but it is their duty to "come out and be separate" from her, and to unite themselves with the true Church of Christ, or the citizens of the heavenly Jerusalem, both in spiritual character and in visible profession.

This, then, is the great practical conclusion at which I have arrived, with reference to my own position and duty; and with this conviction, I have little difficulty in deciding as to the particular branch of the Universal Church which I ought to join. To be a Christian *in the abstract*, without joining any particular Church in preference to another, may seem fair in *theory*, but it is quite inapplicable to *practice*. It is true that there is no Church on earth now, which is *in all respects* the same with the Primitive Church in the days of the Apostles : and yet the Primitive Church is certainly *represented* somewhere at the present day, in its essential features, though not in its accidental circumstances. I am, then, in the first place, a Christian—that is, a member of the Universal, or Catholic Church of Christ ; then, in the second place, believing that the Church of Rome has erred from the truth of the Gospel, I am a member of the Reformed, or Protestant portion of the Christian Church ; and in the third place, being convinced that the Church of England, with all her imperfections, is a sound branch of the Catholic Church of Christ, I desire to return to her communion, because I am satisfied that she is rightly reformed, according to the Word of God, and the doctrine of the Primitive Church, and that she possesses the highest claims on our veneration and obedience, among the Protestant Churches of Christendom. Whatever advantages the Church of Rome may have over Protestant Dissenters, on the ground of Apostolical succession and an ancient Liturgy, the Church of England certainly possesses the same advantages ; and whatever advantages Protestant Dissenters may have over the Church of Rome, on the ground of Scriptural purity of doctrine and worship, the Church of England may fairly claim the same advantages ; and thus she happily combines Evangelical truth with Apostolical order, in her Ecclesiastical constitution. Indeed, as to the uninterrupted succession of Bishops in the national Church of the mother country, she admits of no competition whatever. It has been truly observed that "the orthodox and undoubted Bishops of Great Britain and Ireland are the only persons who, in any manner, whether by ordination or possession, can prove their descent from the ancient Saints and Bishops of these Isles. It is a positive fact, that they, and they *alone*, can trace their Ordinations from Peter and Paul, through Patrick, Augustine, Theodore, Colman, Columba, David, Cuthbert, Chad, Anselm, Osmund, and all the other worthies of our Church. No Popish Bishops can by any possibility trace their spiritual descent by ordination from the original pastors of our Churches ; for their line of succession began at Rome, scarcely more than two Centuries ago ; and none of them have ever received Ordination from any British or Irish Bishops, descended from the ancient line of Prelates, who for so many ages have represented the Apostles in these realms."*

I must observe, however, that I speak of the Church of England as an Ecclesiastical body or religious Society, and not as a political institution or national Establishment. This is a distinction of the utmost importance ; as almost all the objections to the Reformed English Church are founded upon certain historical facts relating to the latter view; whereas the truth of a religion must be considered as altogether independent of its connexion with the State; though it must be confessed that a considerable prejudice naturally arises from attending chiefly to the character and motives of the English statesmen who were instrumental in establishing the change of religion in the country.

It must be admitted that, in an Ecclesiastical point of view, there were some defects and irregularities in the legal Establishment of the English Reformation at the accession of Queen Elizabeth ; but these arose from the peculiar circumstances of the times, and cannot affect the

* Palmer's Origines Liturgicæ, Vol. II. p. 252. (Ed. 1839.)

truth of the doctrines held by the Church of England. It is quite true that the Bishops and Convocation adhered to the Church of Rome, while a majority in Parliament, together with the great body of the Laity and inferior Clergy, supported the Reformation. There were, however, twelve Bishoprics vacant at that time; and what other course could be expected from the remaining fourteen Prelates, who were almost all appointed by Queen Mary, and strongly attached to the See of Rome? These men, together with the Clergy in Convocation, were not properly the representatives of the *national Church* of England, but only of the *Roman branch* of it; and being themselves interested parties in the discussion, their votes cannot be regarded as possessing much weight in matters of controversy. No reformation of doctrine could be effected under the hierarchy of a Church, whose very existence is founded on the impossibility of any such reformation; and therefore, if the Church of England were to be reformed at all, it must be effected, independently of Roman influence, by her own members of the Clergy and Laity, assembled in free deliberation for this purpose; while the external impediments to its progress could only be successfully removed by Parliamentary legislation. And it was certainly accomplished with much wisdom and moderation—first, by the Act of Supremacy, which professed to "restore to the Crown the ancient jurisdiction over the State Ecclesiastical": then by the Act of Uniformity, which enforced the use of the English Liturgy; and finally, by the proceedings of Convocation, which adopted the Thirty-nine Articles as a standard of doctrine. After all, however, the cause of the Reformation must be decided by the truth of its doctrines, and not by the votes of a national Assembly, whether in Parliament or Convocation, which has frequently rescinded its

own former acts, and can only declare the opinions of its
individual members, while it has no power to alter the
nature of divine truth, or to bind the consciences of men
by its decisions in matters of faith.

It cannot be denied that the Royal Supremacy, in
Ecclesiastical causes, was carried to a most unwarrantabl·
extent by the Sovereigns of the House of Tudor, and tha.
it is still frequently asserted in such a sense as to interfere
with the Supremacy of Jesus Christ as the only Head of
His Church. We may, indeed, prefer a total separation
between the Church and State, in *theory*, as better calculated to maintain the spiritual independence of the Church,
to emancipate her from the bondage of State subjection,
and to preserve her from being enslaved by the schemes of
worldly politicians ; but so long as the Supremacy of the
Crown is limited to the *external* government of the Church,
and does not encroach upon her *spiritual* liberties in doctrine and worship, I do not believe that there is any just
cause of objection to the Church of England, on account
of her peculiar relations to the State.

And we have reason to bless God that she never was in
such a high degree of spiritual efficiency as at the present
day ; never before did she possess such a faithful body of
Bishops, Pastors, and lay members in every rank of life,
so distinguished for earnest piety, sound learning, and
laborious zeal in advancing the interests of true religion ;
never did her light shine so brightly, at home or abroad,
in diffusing the saving knowledge of the Gospel among all
classes of the population, in the British dominions, as well
as in heathen lands. And while we cordially acknowledge
her claims, and desire to promote her extension, we feel
that our attachment to her communion, based as it is upon
an intelligent conviction of the Scriptural character of her

doctrines, is by no means of an exclusive or intolerant nature, as it is perfectly consistent with the exercise of universal Christian sympathy, in the most comprehensive sense, with "all them that love our Lord Jesus Christ in sincerity."

Such, then, are the reflections which have long occupied my mind, and which form the substance of my own reasons for deciding in favor of the Protestant religion and the Church of England; and I may here remark that the preceding "Thoughts" were committed to writing, and sent to the press, before I had formally renounced the Church of Rome, and thus they express the gradual progress of my convictions on this important subject. I must confess, indeed, that this whole dispensation is very mysterious to me, as I find it difficult to reconcile it with the promises of God to those who sincerely desire to know and to do His will. Certainly I am not distinctly conscious of any unworthy motives, either in joining, or in leaving, the Church of Rome, as I believed that, in each case, I was guided by the Word and Spirit of God, in answer to prayer. Yet these opposite conclusions could not both have been directly suggested by the Spirit of Truth. I cannot doubt, then, that there must have been some adequate cause for these temptations in myself—some peculiar defect, either in my intellectual constitution or in my religious character, which rendered them needful for me. We are quite sure that all good comes from God, and that all evil comes from ourselves. Perhaps there was some spiritual disease, deeply rooted in my heart, which required such a painful remedy to effect its eradication. Perhaps I was too much absorbed in my beloved studies, and ventured too far into the thorny mazes of theological controversy, which tended only to perplex my mind, while it led to a comparative neglect of the more important practical duties of the Ministry ; and thus God was pleased to leave me for a time to the consequences of my own presumptuous researches, so that I was deceived with the abstract idea of perfect unity, while I was searching for the living unity of an Infallible Church. There can be no doubt ▓▓▓▓ all this was permitted, in some way, for the trial of ▓▓ faith, "to humble me and to prove me." But while we cannot fully comprehend the mysteries of the divine dealings, still "we know that all things work together for good to them that love God;" and with the sweet assurance that "the love of God is shed abroad in our hearts by the Holy Ghost," producing a responsive feeling of love to Him who first loved us, we may rest ▓▓▓ied with all the inexplicable difficulties of the divine ▓▓ment in providence and in grace, and leave the final ▓▓tion with Him who has said, "What I do thou knowest not now, but thou shalt know hereafter."

In conclusion, then, I desire humbly to commit this little work to the blessing of Almighty God, beseeching Him, for Christ's sake, to pardon whatever I may have written in it, or in any other pamphlet, through ignorance or error, which is not in perfect accordance with His holy Word ; and praying that He would graciously be pleased to make it an instrument for the edification of His Church, and the diffusion of true religion among us, "that God in all things may be glorified, through Jesus Christ, to whom be praise and dominion for ever and ever. Amen."